Good for You, Great for Me

GOOD FOR YOU, GREAT FOR ME

Finding the Trading Zone *and* Winning at Win-Win Negotiation

LAWRENCE SUSSKIND

Co-Founder, Program on Negotiation at Harvard Law School,
and Founder of the Consensus Building Institute

PublicAffairs
New York

PublicAffairs books are available at special discounts for bulk purchases in
the U.S. by corporations, institutions, and other organizations. For more
information, please contact the Special Markets Department at the Perseus
Books Group, 2300 Chestnut Street, Suite 200, Philadelphia, PA 19103, call
(800) 810-4145, ext. 5000, or e-mail special.markets@perseusbooks.com.

Book Design by Jack Lenzo

Library of Congress Cataloging-in-Publication Data
Susskind, Lawrence.
  Good for you, great for me : finding the trading zone and winning at win-win
negotiation / Lawrence Susskind—First edition.
      pages cm
  Includes bibliographical references and index.
  ISBN 978-1-61039-425-3 (hardcover)—ISBN 978-1-61039-426-0 (e-book) 1.
Negotiation in business. I. Title.
  HD58.6.S87 2014
  658.4'052--dc23
                              2013050425

ISBN 978-1-61039-524-3 (international edition)
First Edition
10 9 8 7 6 5 4 3 2 1

*To all of my students
from whom I have learned so much*

CONTENTS

Good for You, Great for Me

FINDING THE TRADING ZONE
AT GOLDEN POND

MY WIFE, LESLIE, came dashing up from the beach. We were renting a small cottage by a lake in New Hampshire. For us it was Golden Pond, an idyllic place to spend time with our two young children. We managed to scrape together just enough to afford a two-week vacation.

"You'll never guess who I was just talking to," she gushed. "Ralph. He says that they are selling the cottage. Their son is getting divorced. He wants to cash out his share of the property. I told him we would absolutely buy the place."

I thought for a moment. "How much are they asking?"

"I don't know," she said. "I told him you were the negotiator and you would handle the details."

My mind raced. I could certainly see myself spending a lot more time by the lake, but could we afford it? What had Leslie promised? Owning the cottage would be terrific, but what was Ralph's asking price? I had nothing to go on. I tried to estimate what the annual rental income would be if we bought the cabin but didn't live in it. My back-of-the-envelope estimate (based on the rent we were paying) was that we could clear about $15,000 each year after taxes and expenses. At prevailing interest rates, calculating very quickly, we could use that money to cover a mortgage of about $85,000.

When I talked with Ralph later that afternoon, there was an ironic smile on his face. He knew I was boxed in. "You've been great tenants, and we know how much you love the place. We were delighted when Leslie said you wanted to buy it." I thought to myself, "What has Leslie gotten me into?"

"What's the price?" I ventured.

"We'll be very sad to leave," he said. "Since none of the cabins has sold since the original owners bought them seven years ago, it's hard to know what they're worth. With the common land owned by the lake association, it makes it hard to calculate the actual value of each cottage. In addition to your own cottage, you know, you'll own one ninth of the lake." I could feel his eyes boring into me.

"$105,000," he said. "I think that's really fair. We're glad to be selling the cabin to people who love the place as much as we do. And, it's only 90 minutes from Boston. You'll get to use it all the time."

Ralph and I both knew that Leslie had more or less made a commitment. I would have to find a way to finance the purchase. He was the business manager for a famous magazine and a highly experienced negotiator. I was just starting out. His wife, a local real estate agent, had been quite firm when Leslie made the original deal with her to rent their cottage. I felt trapped, but excited. I had no time to talk to anyone. Could we handle a second mortgage? Could we swing a $20,000 down payment by refinancing our primary mortgage?

"Ralph," I said. "Since you are moving out of state, would you be willing to leave the current furnishings, and include them in the sale price?" "Done," he said. (I figured that would save me about $10,000.) That felt like a victory. I could see a deal taking shape. Presumably I could get an $85,000 mortgage, find $20,000 for the down payment, and avoid the cost of having to furnish the place.

I've always wondered whether he really had $105,000 (or even less) in mind as his final selling price. Unfortunately, I never asked the questions that would have allowed me to find out. I was in too much of a rush to close the deal. I didn't try to imagine the speech he would have to give to his wife and son to be able to declare victory.

Once Ralph talked to Leslie, and she indicated that we would buy the cabin, we were in what I call the "trading zone." That is, both of us had reason to be optimistic there was a deal to be done. He was under a lot of pressure from his "back table," and Leslie had her heart set on a family future by the lake, putting pressure on me. I had no idea what the cottage was worth on the open market. I was sure, though, that if I didn't close the deal quickly another buyer would swoop in and take the cottage from us. You enter the trading zone when both sides begin to believe that a "deal space" exists between the lowest amount one side is ready to accept and the highest amount the other side is willing to pay (or can afford).

In one sense, the trading zone is a state of mind. If both sides are optimistic about reaching an agreement, there's a good chance they will succeed. Of course, how they interact is important. If Ralph had opened with an entirely unreasonable demand, I would have had to walk away and disappoint my wife. If we hadn't paid attention to what the other side wanted and needed, we might have slipped right out of the trading zone. So the trading zone is not just a state of mind, it is an actual deal space circumscribed in very specific ways.

· · · · ·

I DIDN'T HANDLE THE PRESSURE of the negotiation very well. I was in too much of a rush. I should have slowed everything down and found a way to do a lot more homework. I should have asked more questions to determine Ralph's lower limit and to gauge the pressure he was under to get the deal done. Might he have been willing to drop the price another $10,000 if I agreed to sign a letter of intent that afternoon? On the other hand, I knew Leslie would be terribly disappointed if the cottage slipped through our fingers. There were probably a dozen other summer renters ready to buy the cottage (or maybe rent from us if we bought it) as soon as word got out that the unit was for sale. At least, that's what I told myself.

Once you are in the trading zone, and the parties are more relaxed about reaching a deal, the chances of reaching a mutually advantageous outcome increase exponentially. The whole point of getting into the trading zone is that information is more likely to be shared that allows both sides to meet their interests at the lowest possible cost. By exploring lots of options, or potential trades, the parties are more likely to do better for themselves, with less tension and a lower risk of failure than would otherwise be the case.

Unfortunately, I never took advantage of the fact that we were in the trading zone. I never pushed to see how low Ralph would go. He anchored the conversation with his opening bid of $105,000, and I figured Leslie and I could probably borrow that much money. I was able to sweeten the deal a bit by getting him to leave the furnishings, which we liked and he probably had no use for anyway. I assumed he was under some pressure to move quickly, but he never let on that he was eager to close the deal with me in particular. I'm sure he had to report back to his son, Mark, who was half-owner of the cottage. I should have asked to talk with Mark; maybe he would have taken less to get the deal done.

Twenty-five years later, Golden Pond is still our home away from home. My kids want their kids to have the same life-long summer experiences they've had there. Today, the property is worth at least three times what I paid for it. Ralph got a deal that was good for him at the time. It turned out to be great for me in the long run. My Golden Pond experience has taught me a number of lessons. At the top of the list is the realization that if both my negotiating partner and I can get into the trading zone (both the state of mind and the actual deal space), my chances of doing exceptionally well for myself are increased. That is, once I am in the trading zone—which takes some effort on both sides—my chances of winning at win-win negotiation go up. I wish I had been more aware of that when I was negotiating for the cottage; at least I can now share what I've learned.

· · · · ·

THERE IS ALMOST ALWAYS A WAY to find the trading zone if there is one. It requires formulating a deal you can explain to your "back table" (the people to whom you report), and aiming to do well for yourself regardless of how tough your negotiating partner is. Landing deals that are great for you means getting into the right frame of mind, exploring the scope of the deal space, and being ready to claim a disproportionate share of the value you create—something I certainly didn't do when I was negotiating to purchase the cottage at Golden Pond. The same dynamics apply, by the way, in multi-billion-dollar business deals and in small-scale family transactions.

Winning involves three important factors: making sure that

1. the people at your back table are satisfied,
2. you can convince yourself and others that you have been treated fairly, and
3. you generate as much value as possible and use it to produce an agreement that is good for them and great for you.

All of this is a departure from the conventional wisdom about win-win negotiation. Ever since the idea of win-win emerged, and cooperation began to receive as much attention as competition, negotiators have been uneasy about pushing too hard to claim a disproportionate share of the value they create. Not only am I saying that *winning* is OK, but I'm ready to describe how it can be done without violating trust or undermining good working relationships.

A SHIFT IN THE FIELD OF NEGOTIATION

THE WAY PEOPLE THOUGHT ABOUT NEGOTIATION—and actually negotiated—took a significant turn in the 1980s. The focus shifted from knowing how to dominate opponents in all kinds of bargaining situations—in court, business, international relations, and public affairs—to finding some way of convincing your negotiating partners to accept a mutually beneficial—that is, a pretty good—outcome for all sides. This came to be understood as a shift from "win-lose" to "win-win."

While a great many thinkers and writers contributed to this shift in thinking, Roger Fisher, William Ury, and Bruce Patton, authors of *Getting to Yes*, are the best known. Four of their insights are familiar to every experienced negotiator: (1) Don't stint on preparation. It is especially important to clarify ahead of time what you will be left with if there is no agreement. (2) Focus on what's really important to the other side (their interests) rather than any inflated claims or positional statements they might make. (3) Set aside time in every negotiation to brainstorm mutually advantageous options or packages before trying to nail down final commitments. (4) Instead of threats, appeal to rational arguments or what are known as "objective standards" such as "What would an independent expert say that would help me justify my claim that I should get the larger piece of the pie?" A whole training industry now teaches executives and managers how to put these four principles into action and move from win-lose to win–win negotiation.

Millions of people all over the world were swept up in this shift. There is, however, a problem.

Once everyone realized that mutually advantageous outcomes were possible, they were confused. (Millions of people read *Getting to Yes* and other books using the win-win framework, but so did the people on the other side of the bargaining table.) How were they supposed to split the value created when they adopted a mutual gains, or win-win, approach to negotiation? In win-win, is everything supposed to be divided evenly? Is that fair? If one side brings more to the table, shouldn't they get a larger piece of the pie? If one side is more powerful, won't their back table expect them to exploit their leverage and bring home a substantial victory? How can a more powerful negotiator explain why they allowed their negotiating partner to do so well?

A second problem was that having learned the cooperative moves of win-win negotiating, many negotiators were not ready to entirely abandon the competitive instincts that had enabled them to achieve good results in the past. Even the most committed win-win negotiators retain a desire to show their back table they can get a very good outcome—and that, of course, is reasonable. While some negotiators worry they will be betraying the win-win ideal if they try to do especially well for themselves, I don't think they should feel guilty. I think it is possible to adopt a win-win approach *and* do especially well for yourself.

Many negotiation experts are quiet on this issue, urging everyone to be aware of the tension that exists between creating and claiming value. That is, there seems to be a conflict between trying to get as much as possible for everyone while trying to get the most for yourself. They are not explicit, though, about how this tension should be handled. No one has been clear about how much to claim for yourself when adopting a win-win orientation.

If I had had my wits about me when I was negotiating to buy the cottage at Golden Pond, and I had been able to discover that Ralph was ready to accept as little as $70,000 as long as the deal was finalized that day, I would have happily paid the $70,000 *and* asked for the $10,000 worth of furniture. I would not have been troubled by the fact that I had initially been prepared to pay $100,000. If Ralph had promised his son and his wife that he would secure twice what they had paid for the cabin seven years earlier (which I later discovered was $35,000), the deal space would have been between $70,000 and $105,000. I didn't feel any obligation to split the difference (i.e., pay $87,500) or pay the full $105,000 because I was about to get a great long-term deal. Indeed, I would have been comfortable claiming the whole $35,000—paying Ralph $70,000—if I had been clever enough to determine that was how low he was prepared to go.

I was quickly in the trading zone with Ralph because Leslie put me there; however, I didn't have the tools or strategies required to win at win-win negotiation.

Good for You, Great for Me bridges the gap between what people think win-win negotiation requires and what they need to succeed. It offers both principles and strategies—six operational moves you can make once you've found your way into the trading zone—that will allow you to claim as large a share as possible of the value you help create. And it shows how this can be done without undermining trust or ruining relationships. The principles are very straightforward:

1. Lead them into the trading zone.
2. Create more value.
3. Expect the unexpected.
4. Write their victory speech.
5. Protect yourself.
6. Provide leadership.

The strategies offer a means of operationalizing these principles in any negotiation.

Good for You, Great for Me also offers guidance for handling special negotiating circumstances like huge power differentials, relationships that are too important to lose, cross-cultural dynamics, an angry public, and situations where someone appears to be lying.

THE SIX STRATEGIES FOR CREATING DEALS THAT ARE
GOOD FOR THEM AND GREAT FOR YOU

Reframe your negotiating partner's mandate and priorities. There are simple moves you can make to press your negotiating partners to reprioritize their interests. If they aren't clear about their objectives or are coping with mixed messages from their back table, you can help them reframe their interests in a way that will benefit both of you. You can also raise doubts in their minds about what their back tables want from them. Your goal should be to get them to refine their mandate and think hard about their priorities in ways that will benefit both of you. For example, if you put two rather different but attractive proposals forward at the same time—both of which are acceptable to you—it may force your negotiating partner's back table to clarify their priorities. By asking the right questions, you can push your counterparts to seek a mandate that is more advantageous to you.

Propose packages that are good for them and great for you. The key to creating value is inventing trades beneficial to both sides. (That's why it is called the trading zone!) The more value you can create, the more there is to go around; reliable research clearly shows that most negotiators stop far short of generating as much value as possible because they overlook less obvious trades. I demonstrate how to formulate and present trades that the other side cannot afford to turn down, but that are advantageous to you.

Use contingent offers to claim more than the other side. When both sides are clear about the point at which they should walk away rather than accept a bad deal, they can place clear limits on the size of the deal space. Of course, each side wants to be at the edge of the deal space that is most advantageous to them. By using contingent offers (what-if proposals), you can figure out how close you are to the edge that is best for you.

Help the other side sell your best deal to their back table. Too many people see negotiating partners as adversaries when they are in fact important emissaries to back tables. There are simple techniques for providing an emissary with the arguments they need to sell an agreement that is best for you to their back table, the people you usually don't have an opportunity to speak with directly.

Insulate agreements against predictable surprises. Negotiations are not finished until all commitments specified in an agreement are fulfilled. During the follow-up period after an agreement has been signed, lots can go wrong. Market conditions, for example, might change between the time an agreement is reached and the time contractual commitments must be honored. My Harvard Business School colleague Max Bazerman has made it clear that negotiators ought to be able to anticipate the many things that can undermine implementation of a negotiated agreement. It is not that hard to think of the kinds of things that can go wrong, even if we can't predict which one will occur. That's why Bazerman calls them "predictable surprises." Dispute resolution mechanisms can be incorporated into agreements to insulate against some unpredictable surprises. You need to buffer agreements against such surprises, so I outline ways to make your agreements more robust.

Building your organization's negotiating capabilities (so winning at win–win negotiation gets easier over time). Negotiation is as much an organizational task as it is an individual one; and most negotiators know that other people in their company can get in the way of their negotiating efforts. Every time you complete a negotiation, let the relevant people in your organization know how the company's standard operating procedures might be modified to make it easier to find the trading zone and win at win-win negotiation in subsequent negotiations. When negotiators skip this step, everyone in their organization is doomed to generating poorer results in the future.

Six Ways of Winning at Win-Win Negotiation

LEAD THEM INTO THE TRADING ZONE

Help Your Negotiating Partners Reframe Their Mandate and Priorities

THE WORLD ABOUNDS WITH DIFFICULT PEOPLE; and the various difficulties they pose are enhanced when they are negotiating with you. There are the stubborn and the irrational; those who have more power than you and aren't hesitant to use it; the intransigent; and those who absolutely, positively never will allow anything to be built in their back yard. Is it really possible to treat people like this as partners and move them into the trading zone to create deals good for them and great for you?

DEALING WITH STUBBORN OR IRRATIONAL PARTNERS

SUPPOSE YOU'RE AN EXPERIENCED SALESPERSON entering into negotiations for a contract renewal with "Enterprise, Inc.," a company you've successfully done business with for years. Unfortunately, Sue, the head of purchasing at Enterprise, has just been replaced (the memo about her departure noted that she was leaving "to pursue other exciting personal interests"). You call Joe, the new guy, to set up your first meeting and immediately realize you're in for some trouble.

"Here are my rules," Joe says, cutting the pleasantries short. "First, we'll meet at my office. Second, I'll let you know what we will talk about and what we won't. Third, I'll tell you the price range we'll be working in. And we won't put anything in writing until we have a deal."

"I'm fine with meeting at your place," you say uneasily, putting off his other demands for the moment. "But we should probably include some of my production people and someone from your operations division. We've got to make sure we meet their interests as well."

"No," Joe says. "That's not how I do it."

"For years," you continue, "your predecessor always brought along your head of operations. I think that's why everything always went so smoothly. We need to talk about more than just price. We want to make sure that our components meet your company's unique needs."

"Let me worry about that," Joe says.

You are completely taken aback. Joe seems impossible to deal with. Is he truly irrational or just trying to drive a hard bargain? Is he interpreting his mandate too narrowly? Is he clear about his back table's or his company's interests? How can you find out for sure?

One of the trickiest aspects of negotiation is figuring out how to deal with an individual who cannot be convinced by the merits of evidence or arguments. How can you put a stop to irrational behaviors and demands—those that don't appear to contribute at all to the effectiveness of a negotiation? How can you get someone to be reasonable? How do you move someone like this into the trading zone? We'll look at how this story of the new purchasing agent can help you analyze the various possibilities you face when confronting an adversary who seems stubborn, irrational, or even downright crazy. Obviously, you can't win at win-win negotiation unless you figure this out and find a way to move them into the trading zone.

Your negotiating partner is perfectly rational; it's just that you don't understand how the world looks to him. One of the first rules of negotiation is to assume that your partner is rational. Approach each new negotiation with an open mind. Differences in life experience may lead to what look like strange behaviors, so instead of jumping to conclusions, try to imagine how the negotiation might look to the other side. Max Bazerman, the psychologist at Harvard Business School I mentioned earlier, has described many of the cognitive biases that can lead people to read and react to the same situation in totally different ways.

When faced with a partner as stubborn as Joe, imagine what might be going on in his head. Perhaps he's dealing with some new corporate guidelines that govern how he is supposed to proceed. Maybe he's been burned in the past because he wasn't able to manage his internal negotiations while proceeding with external negotiations simultaneously. Perhaps he's nervous about having his performance judged negatively by others in his organization.

How can you address such concerns? First, try asking directly what problem your new partner is trying to solve. "I know you may be feeling some heat back at the office," you might say. "Maybe if I understand what you're up against, we can add some new items to the equation." You might offer to help Joe protect himself, such as by promising to circulate a draft summary of any tentative agreement to both sides. This wouldn't create problems for you and it might help Joe.

Second, you might agree to a couple of Joe's demands, while reserving the right to pause the conversation if they turn out to be counterproductive. Sometimes you might have to try proceeding in a new way, even if it feels unproductive. At the very least, an ongoing failure to move talks forward will provide a shared basis for arguing on behalf of a better approach. As long as you don't agree to anything that fails to meet your company's interests, you won't lose anything by agreeing to what appear to be unproductive demands.

Suppose you agree to meet Joe one-on-one at his office, and you start off the talks like this: "We clearly have common interests. Your company needs our components to stay competitive globally. We're prepared to keep providing them, as long as you maintain or increase your current order. As you know, we have to make continual adjustments in our production systems to get you just what you want, when you want it. If I can come back to my people with a minimum five-year deal, at stable or increasing sales volumes, we can probably remain at the current price with only modest annual adjustments for inflation. What do you think?"

"No way, no how," says Joe, crossing his arms.

"What do you mean?"

"I'm not interested in doing business if you can't give us a substantial reduction in the current unit price," Joe says. "Also, we need to be able to adjust our order up or down. We also want the right to abandon the contract at any time, with no penalty. And you'll have to guarantee on-time delivery or else pay a big penalty."

"Wait a minute, wait a minute," you say. "A penalty if delivery gets held up for reasons beyond our control? A reduction

in unit price? Unpredictable sales volumes? Where is this coming from? No one is paying less than you are for our components. But sales volumes will have to remain constant at least or
we can't provide customized service."

"If you want to keep our business, you'll have to find a
way to cut prices and eliminate any delivery risk," says Joe.
"Now, listen. I promised my guys that we'd have something
signed by now. What's it gonna be?"

"Look," you say. "Our companies have been working together for almost a decade. We ought to be able to sort this out.
Your predecessor and I always put all our cards on the table.
What's going on? Is there some problem you're not telling me
about?"

"I'm sure you and Sue got along great, but times have
changed. Gotta get the price down. Gotta reduce the risk.
Gotta maintain flexibility. Those are the rules. Do we have a
deal, or not?" Joe faces you with a smug smile on his face.

**Your partner is perfectly rational but has adopted a
seemingly irrational stance as part of his hard-bargaining
strategy.** Joe may just be pushing to see what he can get away
with. If you don't push back, he'll keep claiming even more. This
strategy is not irrational, especially for someone who has used it
successfully in the past.

My Golden Rule of Negotiation says that you should treat
your partner the way you'd like to be treated yourself. Negotiation theory suggests that you focus on interests, not positions; separate inventing from committing; invest heavily in
what-if questions; insist on objective criteria; and try to build
nearly self-enforcing agreements. This advice does not preclude

making it clear that there are limits beyond which you will not be pushed. "If you can't be more flexible, we're done," you might tell Joe. "No one is going to give you a better product and better service at a lower price. But if you want to look around, go ahead; then get back to me."

If modeling effective behavior doesn't cause your difficult partner to act reasonably, don't despair. There are several other tactics you can try. First, to test your interpretation of events, insist on bringing others from your organization into the negotiation and press your partner to bring in colleagues as well. In addition, be sure to summarize what's said in writing and distribute memos after each exchange. By doing so, you'll put your difficult partner on notice that others will be aware of what he's up to. Next, put forward multiple proposals that meet your interests very well and that seem to meet the other side's interests at least reasonably well. Even if you don't reach a deal, your offers will be on record. Finally, never make unilateral concessions just to appease your partner. You'll only encourage more of the same unproductive claiming behavior.

Once Joe realizes that there are, indeed, limits to how far he can push you, he may very well temper his demands: "I know you guys do a pretty good job, but there's always room for improvement, right? How are you going to get me a better deal?"

Your partner really is irrational. If so, all rules of normal discourse go out the window. Suppose you've tried all of the strategies outlined above, but they've failed. Joe refuses to listen to your mutually beneficial proposals and won't be convinced by arguments on their merits. Now you're convinced that you are dealing with a truly irrational negotiating partner, someone willing to risk everything to make sure you get nothing. What can you do?

First, prepare a written memorandum laying out several possible deals, and then set an explicit deadline for ending negotiations. Make sure to enumerate all of the evidence and arguments to back up what you are proposing, and spell out why your proposals meet both sides' interests. Though it can be difficult, try to get the memo into the hands of your partner's higher-ups.

If Joe refuses to make progress in your one-on-one exchange, fails to respond to a reasonable set of proposals, and remains unwilling to allow others to attend the negotiations, there's not much reason to go forward. Through his statements, he has signaled a commitment to hard bargaining for its own sake. You've made a number of mutually advantageous proposals, and you're still getting nowhere. It's time to call off the game, break off talks, and wait to see whether Joe will suddenly back down, as hard bargainers sometimes do.

WHEN YOUR NEGOTIATION PARTNER SEEMS IRRATIONAL:

- *Don't respond to irrational behavior in kind*
- *Don't make unilateral concessions to win them over*
- *Don't lose your cool out of frustration*
- *Focus on meeting your own interests*
- *Prepare carefully for each interaction*
- *Summarize each negotiation exchange in writing*
- *Know when it's time to walk away*

Personally, I don't believe that what we assume to be irrational behavior truly is irrational most of the time. Rather, experience tells me it's more likely that people behave according to Possibility #2: they're trying to advance their interests by shutting down the other side through hard bargaining. They may simply be bad negotiators, not irrational ones. In the final analysis, negotiating with a seemingly irrational partner isn't so different from negotiating with anyone else you hope to lead into the trading zone, where great deals might emerge. Going around a negotiating counterpart to their back table may be the only way to help your negotiating partner get a change in their mandate or their organization's priorities.

Sometimes, the best way of dealing with a negotiating partner who has adopted an irrational negotiating posture is to confront them with the facts and, if possible, try to involve them in a process of joint fact-finding.

FIRST, FIND THE FACTS

LET'S LOOK AT A SITUATION that is all too familiar: "The Anaconda Company," a major manufacturer of computer chips, wants to build a new facility on the outskirts of a large city. Both the abutters (the people who live in the area) and regulators demand evidence that the new plant will not increase pollution or diminish property values. Anaconda's management responds by hiring consultants who produce studies backing its claim that the plant's negative impact on the area will be small, if in fact negative at all. Plus, the consultants cite the promise of positive economic impact, especially the creation of jobs. In the meantime, the abutters, fearful of potential health risks and financial losses, hire their own consultants, who produce a report finding that the plant will indeed pose a host of threats, including tainted water, traffic congestion, and damage to local infrastructure. In subsequent face-to-face negotiations, Anaconda disparages the abutters' findings and presents additional commissioned studies. The abutters' experts counter that the possible risks posed by the new plant require additional study and delay. There doesn't seem much hope that they can find the trading zone, let alone create value for mutual gain.

What's the way out of such a predictable mess? Peter Galison, a professor of physics and the history of science at Harvard University, defines the trading zone as a place where conflicting ideas and methods can merge into a shared understanding. He describes the ways in which scientists in distinct but related fields find a common language, or "interlanguage," that allows them to exchange ideas and work through problems.

But in the brouhaha between Anaconda and the abutters, as in many negotiations, disagreement on facts and forecasts hinders people involved in the negotiation in their efforts to find the trading zone. Negotiators often lack the technical expertise necessary to formulate credible solutions to their disputes or find answers to questions such as: What effects will a specific action, such as a new plant, have on key constituents? How might possible effects be enhanced or mitigated? Talks are likely to remain at a standstill until answers are generated that all parties at the table accept and understand.

The next step in this predictable set of interactions? Too often, a lawsuit. In the worst cases, the parties argue endlessly, often in the press, hiding behind the findings of their respective hired guns. In many quarters this has been dubbed "adversary science." From the public's standpoint, if you can hire a scientist to say whatever you want, why take science into account at all? In some instances, the parties decide to ignore all scientific or technical considerations, since there are none that they trust. This is likely to produce an agreement that meets no one's interests and may even create dangerous and counterproductive results.

MAPPING THE TERRITORY, TOGETHER

SOME MIGHT ARGUE that such confrontations are inevitable. But a wide range of collaborative efforts, many of which I have been involved in personally, have convinced me that the battle of the printout can be avoided. For example, groups for and against large-scale development projects or plant closings have come together to undertake joint investigations of potential impacts. These have led to decisions about whether and how to proceed, and also about what compensation should be paid to those who might be adversely affected.

How can negotiators in situations such as the battle between Anaconda and the abutters find their way quickly and easily into the trading zone? One method I've seen work time and again in a wide variety of negotiations is joint fact-finding, a multistep, collaborative process for bringing together negotiating partners with different interests, values, and disciplinary perspectives. By agreeing on how information will be gathered, analyzed, and interpreted, the parties lay the foundation for subsequent negotiation. Joint fact-finding, which helps maximize joint gains, has proven successful in helping parties resolve disagreements, particularly highly technical ones. While each party will seek to do the best it can for itself, joint fact-finding enables both to transition into the trading zone. As all sides seek to win, their chances of meeting their own interests while simultaneously meeting the interests of other parties will increase.

Unbiased expert advice is key. Without help from experts they all trust, each party remains too focused on its own interests to move together in the right direction.

Joint fact-finding typically proceeds as follows:

Scope the dialogue. People disagreeing about the legitimacy of each other's claims must first reach agreement on the questions and topics to include on their negotiation agenda. In the case of the siting of the manufacturing plant, Anaconda and the abutters need to agree on a list of questions regarding the potential environmental and financial impacts of the facility. Such questions usually provoke an information-gathering process, although parties may not see eye to eye on the methods or the analyses required. How can they resolve these early differences? By setting written ground rules they can all live with.

The simplest way to generate ground rules is to have a trusted intermediary, such as a professional mediator with the appropriate technical background, carry drafts from party to party until they reach agreement. In their ground rules, parties must ensure that all sides have the technical background, or at least access to appropriate technical guidance, necessary to engage in a productive dialogue.

It's useful for the ground rules to establish the amount of time and money participants will devote to data gathering and analysis. They may also include guarantees of confidentiality and clarification of the participants' interests.

Jointly choose expert advisers. Once there is agreement on ground rules and a fact-finding agenda, Anaconda and the abutters are ready to select technical advisers and analytic methods that will deliver the answers they need. If each selects its own advisers, the likely result is the all-too-common situation of conflicting technical inputs and dueling experts. A more effective alternative is jointly selecting a set of neutral technical advisers. (Note another big benefit of joint fact-finding: a shared analysis can literally cut parties' research costs in half.)

But the task of selecting advisers often brings philosophical differences to the fore. In the dispute over the manufacturing plant, Anaconda, motivated to show the financial benefits the plant would bring to the community, might insist on the joint hiring of an economist. For their part, the abutters might push to employ scientists who will focus on potential environmental risks. The solution? They agree to hire an array of advisers adept at working in a multidisciplinary fashion. Many people are surprised to learn that there are experts in a wide range of fields who prefer to operate in a collaborative mode.

Define the appropriate methods of analysis. It is important to ask all advisers to subscribe to the ground rules. They also need to make explicit the assumptions they bring to the task at hand. In the case of the manufacturing plant, the analysts—regardless of their disciplinary backgrounds—need to specify the geographic scope of the area that frames their analysis, for example. A natural scientist might want to look at the larger ecosystem, while an economist might focus on the relevant municipality. Their conclusions cannot be merged until they agree on a set of geographic boundaries for whatever studies need to be done. They also need to make clear the time frame they are using for their analyses, or their separate contributions won't fit together. And they should accept responsibility for making clear the levels of uncertainty built into their analyses. For instance, in forecasting the impact of a new plant on water quality, a great deal will depend on the assumptions made about the chances of a new water treatment system breaking down or being operated improperly. Risk management assumptions can radically alter the forecast of the dangers that might be involved.

If the analysts have a hard time communicating with the parties or with one another, an intermediary with the appropriate technical background may be needed to carry the joint fact-finding process forward.

Clarify roles and responsibilities. Whether negotiations are taking place inside a corporation or in a more public setting, all parties need to meet with their hired technical advisers throughout the entire joint fact-finding process. Joint fact-finding will fail unless open communication exists among technical advisers, the negotiating parties, and each side's constituents.

The jointly chosen advisers may be top experts in their fields, but there are many forms of knowledge that only stakeholders can contribute. In the end, it is the parties themselves who must decide how to act. For this reason, they need to be genuinely engaged with their advisers, but also responsible for drawing their own conclusions.

Assess tentative findings together. Once jointly selected technical advisers have produced the data or analyses requested by Anaconda and the abutters, it's important that the parties engage in a face-to-face exchange to consider what their advisers have produced. Advisers can present various courses of action, highlighting the probable gains and losses associated with each, but decisions should be made by the parties. The analysts should help the parties make sense of the findings by pointing out the extent to which they hinge on critical assumptions. For example, if a team of analysts suggests that the risks associated with the proposed plant are minimal, they need to make clear what they mean. One way to do this is to relate the projected risks to comparable risks that most people choose to accept in their everyday lives. They also need to make explicit what they are assuming about the company's probable response to a system failure, such as its commitment to immediately mitigate any adverse effects that might occur.

By questioning the advisers about their results, Anaconda and the abutters can assure themselves and each other that the joint fact-finding process has indeed answered their questions. The advisers' initial findings are likely to trigger a set of second-order questions, and the parties shouldn't hesitate to send the analysts back to work. Although repeated face-to-face exchanges will be limited by time and money, a collective examination of a range of what-if scenarios is crucial to finding the trading zone.

Note that the analysts' objectivity remains essential even after they've delivered their results. For this reason, they must refrain from recommending any one course of action that might follow from their findings.

Communicate results. In many negotiations, the parties at the table represent large constituencies. Whether the negotiators are corporate employees or neighborhood activists, it's unreasonable to expect them to communicate the results of sophisticated technical analyses to their constituents without help. Instead, their shared technical advisers might present the results of joint fact-finding to each constituency separately, or they

TO WORK TOGETHER TO FIND THE FACTS:

- *Scope the dialogue*
- *Jointly choose expert advisers*
- *Define the appropriate methods of analysis*
- *Clarify roles and responsibilities*
- *Assess tentative findings together*
- *Communicate results*

might put up a website that all participants can use to keep their constituents informed.

What happens next. Responding to the results of joint fact-finding is, of course, the next crucial step. Even if all sides agree that they asked the right questions and that the advisers answered those questions satisfactorily, the leap from ideas to action will always reflect the parties' varied interests. Before they can function effectively in the trading zone, negotiators must confront the ways in which their conflicting preferences cause them to interpret the same data differently.

Having a shared database doesn't mean that Anaconda and the abutters will be able to agree on what needs to be done next. But agreed-upon facts and forecasts do ensure that technical considerations won't be brushed aside. And, if jointly developed facts and forecasts (of potential risks or impacts) suggest that a mandate provided by a back table is based on wrong assumptions, they offer a face-saving way for a negotiator to go back to her organization and ask for a new mandate or a clarification of interests. Joint fact-finding helps disputants guarantee that they've received unbiased technical advice—the very advice they need in order to work effectively in the trading zone.

Now, think about the connection between joint fact-finding, as I've just described it, and the first step in winning at win-win negotiation. If your goal is to get your negotiating partner to reframe their mandate or reprioritize their interests—because if they do so, it would be more advantageous to you—you can use the results of a believable joint fact-finding process to push in this direction.

Let's say I'm the Anaconda representative who has been getting stonewalled by the abutters' lawyer. All along I've said that the risks involved in building the computer chip plant we are proposing are minimal. I know that my claims are suspect in the minds of a frightened community. After agreeing to engage in a joint fact-finding process (with independent experts that my company, the community, and state and local regulators agreed upon), we now have a risk assessment that pretty much confirms what I have been saying. I know there are promises my company can make that will be meaningful to the abutters if they accept the joint fact-finding report. I can ask the lawyer for the abutters to share the report with his client and maybe even encourage them to meet with the members of the joint fact-finding panel. Now, perhaps, we can move into the trading zone.

You can't win at win-win negotiation until you find your way into the trading zone. A joint fact-finding process can help you get there. You can use the results of such a process to suggest that your negotiating partner has too narrow a mandate, too rigid a sense of how their side's interests might be met, or even the wrong idea about what their interests are. Use the results of joint fact-finding to get your counterparts to go to their back table and force a reconsideration of their interests. Here's yet another example of what it may take to move a difficult partner into the trading zone.

NEGOTIATING WITH A 900-POUND GORILLA

DO YOU EVER HAVE TO NEGOTIATE with a behemoth that dominates your market—the so-called 900-pound gorilla—and face being forced to take its offer or be squeezed out of the market? Here's how to expand your options, bring a very powerful negotiating partner into the trading zone, and ultimately win at win-win negotiation.

Whether they're big-box retailers with aggressive pricing strategies or well-established computer software providers, one or two companies seem to set all the rules in many industries today. As a negotiator, your apparent choice is between taking what little the other side offers or being squeezed out of the market entirely.

When there was still one-hour photo processing, that is, before everyone had a digital camera, "PictureQuik" had one-hour processing booths in every U.S. branch of "SuperMart," a huge global discount retail chain. Although the arrangement was profitable for both sides, SuperMart abruptly informed PictureQuik that all the booths were up for grabs in a single national contract renegotiation. PictureQuik knew that its competitors would be ready with lowball bids. If another company took over their thousands of booths, PictureQuik could take a devastating financial hit. Soon after its announcement, SuperMart told PictureQuik, "We have a great offer from one of your competitors. To keep the contract, you'll have to pay us

10 percent more of your in-store revenue and 10 percent more to rent the booths in our stores. Take it or leave it." Now what?

What choices do PictureQuik executives have, aside from accepting whatever SuperMart wants? They can take the deal and impose extreme cost-cutting measures, but that isn't a feasible option. And walking away from their biggest client would be potentially catastrophic.

How should a negotiator in a weak position deal with a seemingly all-powerful opponent? How do you move a 900-pound gorilla like SuperMart into the trading zone? There are three negotiation strategies to use as you think through how to win the negotiation the next time your business confronts an organization like this.

Seek an Elegant Solution

WHEN CONFRONTED WITH an unattractive offer from a powerful competitor, the best way to alter the balance of power may be to seek an elegant solution—a counterproposal that will create even more value for both sides than what the 900-pound gorilla is trying to impose. An elegant solution often exploits the underused resources of one negotiating partner for the benefit of both. Such a solution may require a substantial investment of time, money, and effort—and it doesn't emerge on its own.

How can you generate an elegant solution in your negotiations with a stronger partner? First, to improve your walk-away, think about altering your own business strategy. Specifically, look for low-cost ways to generate greater returns under your current contract. For PictureQuik, this means satisfying SuperMart's revenue goals while increasing its own annual take. PictureQuik might, for instance, consider offering additional products or services at its booths, such as software for creating online photo albums. Or it might seek out a partner to sell related goods or services, such as a company that prints images on photo albums or mouse pads. PictureQuik might then be able to come up with the extra 10 percent that SuperMart is demanding while simultaneously increasing its own profits.

Second, to build an elegant solution, further explore the other side's interests. PictureQuik might, for example, try to identify additional segments of the demographic market that SuperMart wants to bring into its stores. What current Super-Mart product lines are on a downward profitability trend? In what areas is it losing to its competitors? With this information in hand, PictureQuik may be able to help SuperMart solve an existing problem. PictureQuik could make a side deal to distribute a computer game that SuperMart doesn't currently carry but that would appeal to teenagers who don't usually frequent the store. A potential partner seeking a featured spot in SuperMart's stores might be willing to help PictureQuik create an attractive package to present to the retailer. By preparing a range of proposals, PictureQuik could alter the balance of power in its renegotiations with SuperMart.

Third, consider other ways of creating value for the stronger party. Instead of packaging finished photos in its own distinctive envelopes, PictureQuik could switch to a jointly produced envelope that features SuperMart's logo. It could also include SuperMart coupons in every pack of finished photos, or print SuperMart's logo on the back of all finished photos. Through joint branding and other new forms of advertising,

PictureQuik could add value to their partnership, demonstrating that SuperMart would be better off continuing their relationship rather than switching to a competitor.

Appeal to Principle

WHEN A STRONGER PARTY is taking a tough financial stance, it's easy to believe that the negotiation is entirely about price. The fact is, nonmonetary considerations are often more important to one or both negotiating partners than you might expect. You can identify these factors by questioning the other side's team about their interests. Once you've identified the underlying principle that the other party is following, you'll be in a better position to brainstorm problem-solving strategies.

The trick is to determine how the other side is measuring its success, then think of a way to help them meet that goal at the lowest possible cost to you. Here are just a few of the appeals to principle that you might make in a business negotiation:

- We've worked well together in the past—and profitably. Remember, it took some time for us to work out the kinks at the outset. You would be sacrificing reliability if you switched to another provider. Do you see the risk in starting all over again with another company that can't guarantee uniform, reliable performance?
- We know this business better than anyone else. If someone is offering the same service at a lower price, he's lowballing you simply to get in the door. You're going to have a lot of unhappy customers on your hands because the supplier won't be able to deliver quality service at that price. How important is quality to you?

- We have a great working relationship. Some of your stores were delayed in opening, but we were willing to wait. Is our flexibility and loyalty worth something to you?

By appealing to principles of fairness, PictureQuik might be able to identify the standard that SuperMart is applying to all of its in-store partners by asking, "Why should we pay you an additional 10 percent of our in-store revenue? Are you asking all your suppliers for equivalent increases? If not, is it fair of you to single us out?" SuperMart might reveal that it has set new, higher revenue goals for each square foot of every store. If that's the case, PictureQuik could offer to redesign its booths to reduce their size by 10 percent.

It's possible the response to such appeals will be, "Take it or leave it. We have someone else ready to step in." But wise executives recognize the importance of focusing not only on increased short-term profitability but also on solid relationships and consumer satisfaction.

Of course, it's important to present an appeal to principle to the right person. The middle manager with a mandate to get the best deal possible may not be the right audience for such arguments. Whenever you're dealing with a stronger party, nurture contacts with top management on the other side—throughout the life of your partnership. At the moment of contract renegotiation, you won't have the time or the opportunity to build such ties.

Form Strategic Alliances with Your Competitors

THE PREVIOUS TWO STRATEGIES will usually be the most desirable, as they allow you to keep the entire market to yourself.

But it makes sense to explore a third strategy before it becomes clear that the other two won't work on their own.

As the weaker party in a negotiation, you can increase your leverage by forming strategic alliances that undercut your stronger opponent's ability to generate a better offer that excludes you. In the language of negotiation, your goal should be not only to improve your own walk-away option but also to reduce the 900-pound gorilla's walk-away by co-opting the competition.

Imagine that PictureQuik has been anticipating Super-Mart's hard-line bargaining for almost a year before the end of their current contract. In that case, the photo processor could easily identify which competitors would be most likely to bid against it. From its competitors' standpoint, getting a contract with SuperMart would be a major coup, even if they initially made little or no money off the deal. A competitor that re-placed PictureQuik in SuperMart stores could see its share of the photo-processing market climb from 10 percent to 50 per-cent nationally.

Suppose that PictureQuik knows that SuperMart has been seeking to expand its presence in other countries. If so, Picture-Quik could approach Phototime, one of its most likely compet-itors, about making a joint bid to split the retail chain's global market in areas where Phototime is already well established. From Phototime's standpoint, a joint bid would more or less guarantee a larger share of the market. From PictureQuik's standpoint, such a deal would avoid a head-to-head competi-tion with a major competitor and would reduce the risk of be-ing boxed out of the business entirely.

Another option would be to bypass your main competi-tor and approach your next-strongest competitor in pursuit of a partnership with them instead. In this case, PictureQuik, the industry leader, would bypass Phototime and invite the third- or fourth-largest photo-finishing provider to be part of a joint bid to SuperMart. After all, they and a lower-ranked competitor should be able to offer SuperMart a better deal than Phototime could on its own. PictureQuik would supply the inventory needed to move to SuperMart's new stores and train supervisors to oversee expanded operations and employees in global markets. Phototime would have to struggle mightily just to handle existing SuperMart booths.

In an alliance, the combined strength of the partners exceeds the sum of their parts. For this reason, finding a partner that operates in markets where PictureQuik and SuperMart would like to expand could be an ideal solution. Such an arrangement might allow PictureQuik to retain most of their market while letting a competitor control a larger share of its expanding overseas business.

Often, you can expect the 900-pound gorilla to be so confident of its strength that it won't listen to counterarguments. In such circumstances there is no way to win at win-win negotiation. Such a behemoth may not understand the value of focusing on the full range of its own long-term interests. Instead, it may treat each negotiation as an occasion to flex its muscles and defeat weaker opponents. In such situations, your best response may be to seek out the gorilla's handler—members of top management rather than, say, regional sales managers—and put forward an elegant proposal that's better than your existing deal. You might also want to point out the important principles that are at stake, such as reliability and loyalty, and turn the discussion into an inquiry about meeting those standards.

WHEN THE OTHER SIDE IS MORE POWERFUL:

- *Seek an elegant solution*
- *Appeal to principle*
- *Form strategic alliances with your competitors*

OVERCOMING THE NOT–IN–MY–BACKYARD SYNDROME

FOR MORE THAN A DECADE, backers of the Cape Wind project have been seeking to build America's first offshore wind farm. A small but determined and well-funded group of opponents has tried to stop them at every turn. In a National Public Radio story about growing opposition to renewable energy facilities, wind power advocates were asked how they might overcome local opposition—dubbed the "NIMBY syndrome"—in the future. The spokesperson said, "We've got to get in there earlier and educate people." Wrong, I say! How arrogant! You think people are opposed because they don't understand? No, they're opposed because the costs *to* and impacts *on them* are likely to outweigh the likely benefits *to them*. The only way to overcome the NIMBY syndrome, regardless of the type of facility, is to make sure that the overwhelming majority of people in the area know that the benefits *to them* will outweigh the costs and impacts *they* are likely to experience if the facility is built.

Almost every significant construction project starts with a small percentage of people, probably less than 10 percent, who favor whatever is being proposed. These are usually people likely to gain personally if the facility is built, maybe by selling

their land directly to the facility developer. And, as Mike Elliott, a professor at Georgia Tech, demonstrated many years
ago, an equally small percentage of people usually start out opposed. Typically, these are people likely to bear disproportionate costs—maybe because they live right next to whatever is
being proposed. While there are some people in every community who pay no attention to anything (maybe 10 percent),
the vast majority—60–65 percent—fall into a category Elliott
called "Guardians." It's what this middle group does that triggers and shapes the outcome of most facility siting controversies, such as the one involving Cape Wind.

We know two things about Guardians (thanks to Professor
Elliott). First, if they think a licensing or permitting decision is
unfair, they will side with the opponents. Second, they want
to consider the arguments for and against a proposed facility
on their merits. If believable information isn't presented in an
open forum where questions can be asked of experts and proponents in a problem-solving format, Guardians will side with
the opponents. NIMBYism occurs when these two facts about
Guardians are ignored.

Let me get back to the wind energy spokesperson on
NPR. If proponents put out one-sided information to help sell
citizens on the need for new renewable energy facilities, or try
to convince them that there won't be any adverse impacts, that's
sure to backfire. I advocate a different approach that emphasizes
three very different ideas:

1. Engage in joint fact-finding, not one-sided "educational" efforts.
2. Let all the key stakeholders choose a mediator to help
   manage a consensus-building process.

3. Promise to compensate potential losers and hold any
   adversely affected neighborhoods harmless.

Most environmental studies are prepared *after* proponents have committed to building a facility. So whatever data or forecasts are generated tend to be dismissed by opponents as nothing but propaganda in support of decisions that have already been made. This is exactly the kind of thing that causes Guardians to side with the opponents. The Cape Wind project in Massachusetts was caught up for most of the past decade in what must be the most elaborate regulatory review process in energy facility siting history in the United States. Whatever evidence was presented by proponents, though, was countered by opponents. Everyone had made up their minds long before studies of the likely impacts of the facility became available. By the time the formal regulatory reviews took place, it was impossible to get all the parties in the same room for a civil conversation. Maine, however, took a different tack. The state reviewed all possible offshore wind sites before any projects were proposed and noted publically those that seemed to make the most sense in technical, economic, and aesthetic terms. This made it a lot easier for energy industry developers to know where and how they might proceed.

Most public involvement in government decisions in the United States is a joke. Hearings and so-called town meetings offer trivial opportunities for opponents and proponents to make short statements that won't convince anyone of anything. They are all for show. The real battle takes place in the media and behind the scenes as each group does its best to lobby the elected and appointed officials involved.

Only an extended public dialogue, when questions can still be asked and answered, before the Guardians have taken sides, is likely to lead to believable analyses of the merits and demerits of each proposed technology, location, design, or mitigation strategy. Most project proponents know how to do this, but it requires that some of the money that would otherwise be spent on lawyers and litigation be used to pay professional mediators to facilitate authentic problem-solving or consensus-building efforts early on. This is not about public relations (which is what the wind spokesperson meant by "education"). Rather, it's about learning something through an inquiry facilitated by a professional mediator, also called a "neutral." Most people don't even realize that such a thing is possible! Mediators know how to bring the right parties to the table, prepare a jointly crafted agenda, and bring in a range of expert advisers acceptable to all sides to engage in joint fact finding.

Now we get to the third principle. Unless you hold potential losers harmless, they will oppose anything that is likely to hurt them. If you want to build a new facility in a particular location, there is no question that a small number of people living adjacent to the site will be opposed. Trying to get them to support the project by telling them that the gains to everyone else outweigh whatever losses they might experience is crazy. It is too easy for all the potential losers to find each other, especially if there are not that many of them. And they have a substantial incentive to try to block the facility. On the other hand, all the potential gainers (who could number in the millions if we are talking about switching from fossil fuels to clean energy on a regional basis) are unaware of the small gains they might realize over the long haul, so they don't have much of an incentive to get organized.

If the gains to the gainers far outweigh the losses to the losers, that's not going to stop the small number of potential losers from trying to stop something that is not in their best interest. And since regulators and public officials don't think in terms of the distribution of gains and losses , they often play into the hands of a small group of opponents who can easily recruit Guardians by complaining that decisions have been made without them. Instead of 10 percent opposed, the opposition grows to more than 50 percent. When that happens, public officials have no choice but to take a stand against a proposed project.

The key is to help reframe the Guardians' mandate and priorities by offering compensation and commitments to potential losers. If offers of compensation are structured properly, they can lead potential opponents into the trading zone. Compensation doesn't have to take the form of financial payments. For example, a facility developer could promise to help a community fix something that has been a problem for a long time —like cleaning up a contaminated site somewhere else in the area—if they are allowed to build their new facility.

A bribe is an illegal payment which people would be embarrassed to have made public. But compensation, awarded based on clear principles that ensure that everyone in the same category is treated equally, is not a bribe. Community benefit agreements (currently on the books in New York City and Los Angeles) seek to ensure that everyone in a neighborhood will benefit when a new facility of some kind is built. Some of the gains to the gainers (especially proponents who stand to make a profit) are, in effect, taxed (before they go to the gainers) and used to ensure that the small number of opponents who really stand to lose will be made whole. Gains are used to compensate communities who experience real losses so that almost everyone in the city or region benefits. Compensation payments or compensatory measures to eliminate a problem in the area (or share benefits) ensure that all those who bear disproportionate costs (even small ones) realize some tangible advantage over and above the general benefits that all the gainers will get if a facility is built. Construction jobs, for example, ought to be set aside for those adversely affected. Property tax abatements (or at least property tax insurance) should be offered to those who live near a new facility. This will hold them harmless against any property value losses caused by a new facility. The key is to ensure that potential losers are fully compensated. This will lead the Guardians to reframe their priorities and allow them to side with the proponents. When this happens, NIMBYism will melt away.

If there is no way to capture some of the benefits to compensate the losers by taxing the gainers, then the proposed facility is probably a mistake—it's either in the wrong location, using the wrong technology, or being proposed at the wrong time.

Now, there are some opponents who just don't care what they are offered or what their neighborhood is offered (again, I'm not just talking about money). They oppose a new facility for ideological reasons or because they just don't want things to change. In real life, when the ideas I have outlined are followed, the folks in this category (ideological opponents) are a very small minority (fewer than 5 percent of the total population of a community or region). Elected and appointed officials (and courts) who see that every effort has been made to use some gains to compensate losers and make the host community whole (through an open problem-solving conversation managed by a professional mediator) are not likely to block what 95 percent of the community supports. So the trick is to get the Guardians to side with the proponents, bringing them into the trading zone. Once they are there, the next task is to create as much value as possible.

TO GET PAST NIMBYISM:

- *Engage in joint fact-finding, not one-sided "educational" efforts*
- *Let all key stakeholders choose a mediator to help manage the consensus-building process*
- *Promise to compensate potential losers, and hold any adversely affected neighborhoods harmless*

CREATE MORE VALUE

Propose Packages That Are Good for Them and Great for You

CREATING MORE VALUE THROUGH TRADES

DOES YOUR PAST NEGOTIATION EXPERIENCE bear out the optimistic notion that it's possible to uncover hidden value that improves each side's outcomes in virtually every negotiation? Or are you skeptical?

At the Program on Negotiation at Harvard Law School, the mutual-gains approach to negotiation lies at the center of much of the prescriptive advice we offer practitioners. This way of thinking puts a premium on value creation—that is, enlarging the pie before dividing it. Value creation hinges on finding and making trades that allow each party to meet their underlying interests. If the package you invent helps both sides exceed their *best alternative to a negotiated agreement*, it makes sense to do the deal.

Most people agree that value creation sounds like a good idea. Yet many argue that *their* negotiations can't be handled that way, either because their counterparts are too committed to hard bargaining or because no additional value exists. In effect, they presume that most negotiations are zero-sum games in which every bit of gain for one side is matched by a loss to the other, and vice versa.

It's true that finding issues to trade is not always easy. If you are negotiating with one person over just one issue, such as the price of a used computer on eBay, and you're unlikely to have any future dealings with him, you may indeed be hard-pressed to create value.

Most of the time, however, the agenda in any negotiation can be expanded, and items can be packaged. For example, a financial deal that seems to be exclusively based on price (Issue 1) usually also concerns when the money will change hands (Issue 2) and the likely interest rate that will be charged in the interim (Issue 3). Suppose that a salesperson's commission is determined by the price a buyer agrees to pay, and that the amount the buyer is willing to pay depends on when that payment is due. "If you sign the papers now, you won't have to pay for a year," the salesperson seeking a commission might say. "We'll extend you a line of credit at no interest." If the client can't afford the purchase immediately, but knows that she'll have the necessary funds in six months, the two sides can reach a value-creating deal by exploiting their differing rankings of the three issues on the table.

Often it seems as if there is only one issue at stake in a negotiation. But this is rarely the case. For example, if a negotiation is entirely focused on how much something will cost, it is possible to add issues like when payment will be due, how it can be financed, and how payment for one thing can be linked to subsequent purchases or sales. The key is to put together a package that exceeds each party's expectations. Using a wide variety of examples—from negotiating a strategic alliance to resolving conflict that threatened the viability of a business—I'll present four value-creating moves that all negotiators should be ready to use: preparing to create value, exploring interests and adding issues, playing the What-If Game, and bringing new parties to the table.

Prepare to create value. When preparing to negotiate, always take time to consider two important questions from your perspective, as well as that of the other side: What is your walk-away option, and what, in rank order, are your interests? While most negotiators think about them, they do so only from their own perspective. Careful analysis and estimation, as well as conversations with others, can help you answer these questions.

It is important to spend as much time contemplating the other side's walk-away options and interests as you spend thinking about your own. After all, you probably won't be able to propose a package that the other side will accept if you haven't thought through their away-from-the-table options and their most important needs and wants. In addition, be sure you have a mandate from your superiors or partners to explore options for mutual gain. Finally, get ready to propose packages that exceed the other side's walk-away (if only slightly), meet their interests (reasonably well), greatly exceed your walk-away, and elegantly meet your interests.

By preparing to propose multiple packages at the same time, you can avoid having a preliminary offer misconstrued as a final offer. Each package should be designed to test whether your estimates of the deal space are correct. The more extensively you prepare to address the other side's interests, the more value-creating opportunities you are likely to find once talks begin.

Explore interests and add issues. When seated at the bargaining table, what's the best way to uncover your negotiation counterpart's unspoken interests? Ask questions, then listen carefully to his answers. Even if you've decided to make the first offer and are ready with a number of alternatives, the process of asking and listening to assess interests should always come before proposing options.

Note that if your style of listening isn't sufficiently empathetic, it won't elicit honest responses. Furthermore, you'll have to ask a lot of questions to get a clear picture of someone's interests. Also, to model the type of response you're seeking, you must be willing to reveal your *own* interests. All too often many people assume that exposing their interests will give the other side an unfair advantage, but this is rarely true.

If your attempts to uncover the other party's interests fail, even after you've revealed your own, try probing in a different way. Suppose that you ask a potential client, "Are you more concerned about the cost or the quality of the service we are proposing to provide?" His reply: "Both!" You might then ask, "Would you prefer that we assign our most senior staff member to your account, even though her hourly rate is a bit higher than anyone else's? She's one of the best in the field, without a doubt." The client's response will reveal whether he's more concerned about price or quality.

Here's another way to probe the same person's interest: "Other clients have raved about some of our junior people—and we take only the best—assigning them entirely to a single account. This has allowed us to charge a lower hourly rate than usual while giving the client the attention they want. Would you like to talk to some of our clients who have used this approach?"

Value creation can be especially difficult when parties get snagged on an underlying value difference. When this happens, bridge the gap by identifying overarching values that could provide a motivation to work together. Take for example the abutters challenging Anaconda, the manufacturer (see chapter 1), to pay more attention to the health concerns of nearby residents. As a member of Anaconda's management team, rather than arguing that your company has to stay focused on the bottom line, point out that you share the neighbors' commitment to environmental and health improvement. Then consider proposing an effort to replace aging, polluting equipment with more efficient production technologies that will save your firm money in the long run while simultaneously reducing the neighbors' health risk. Such value-creating opportunities can be uncovered by searching for a common interest, such as commitment to health and environmental improvement, rather than letting differences between you dominate the discussion.

Play the What-If Game. The practice of value creation almost always means playing the What-If Game. Specifically, to test whether a trade genuinely creates value, try it out on the other side.

Imagine that you're renegotiating a contract with a customer who is satisfied with the product you currently supply. Your company, however, has invested heavily in a new, improved version of the product, and your own interest lies in persuading the customer to switch to it. By questioning him about his interests, you learn that he's concerned about the rising costs associated with expanding his business. Here's one what-if scenario you might propose: "If I offered you a 10 percent rebate on every new unit you purchase beyond the $50,000 mark, would you be willing to switch to our improved version?"

Assuming you've agreed to brainstorm ideas before putting together a final deal, you can feel comfortable testing a variety of packages. You can further reduce the risk that your customer will assume prematurely that you're ready to make a specific offer by putting forward more than one what-if proposal at a time. "I can either offer you free delivery," you might say before he has had a chance to respond to your first offer, "or give you a 10 percent rebate on orders of the new product that exceed $50,000." The other party's response should reveal which trade he values more. If he appears to value a rebate more than free delivery, follow up with two more proposals: "I could even give you a rebate of 15 percent on orders above $100,000 if you buy the new version of the product, or I can extend the payment due date by three months with no interest." Each package is designed to create a little more value by taking advantage of mutually beneficial trades.

Make no mistake: there comes a time in every negotiation when the value you've created must be divided or distributed. That's the moment when your chance to win arises. Sometimes anxiety about this competitive dimension inhibits negotiators' ability to create value. Sharing information and engaging in empathetic listening may seem like risky behaviors when you anticipate a distributive battle, but I hope I can convince you otherwise.

Bring new parties to the table. What do you do when little or no trust exists between negotiators? Consider recruiting an intermediary, trusted by both sides, to serve as a go-between focused on creating value. This role could be filled by a professional mediator or by someone with whom both sides have worked in the past, such as a banker who has financed earlier deals. The neutral person's duties would include meeting privately with each side, exploring their interests, and helping to identify mutually advantageous trades. Adding a neutral to the negotiation can assist you in overcoming any uneasiness or reluctance about revealing information about your interests. (Both sides retain subsequent deniability if the go-between is unable to suggest value-creating trades.)

When two parties have found little or nothing to trade, they can create value by inviting still more potentially interested parties to participate in the negotiation. Bringing in an additional equity partner, for example, might close a gap between a buyer and a seller, though a third party would likely reduce the original players' profit. Similarly, a company seeking to buy a new technology through its global purchasing department might find that involving its engineering staff in early discussions with the license holder could lead to new ideas about how to test the technology (once it is in the buyer's hands) in ways that will give the seller new performance results and thus greater credibility with a far larger market. While adding parties to a negotiation undoubtedly adds complexity, it can also

---

FOUR VALUE-CREATING MOVES:

- *Prepare to create value*
- *Explore interests and add issues*
- *Play the What-If Game*
- *Bring new parties to the table*

help you enlarge the pie before turning to traditional issues such as cost, delivery, and maintenance.

In sum, remember that situations appearing to be zero-sum rarely are. The key to value creation? Bringing a degree of optimism about the chances of expanding the pie to every negotiation. It is a lot easier to win at win-win negotiation—that is, claim a disproportionate share of the value being distributed—if you have done everything you can to create as much value as possible.

NEGOTIATING STRATEGIC ALLIANCES

WHEN WE CARE A LOT about maintaining important relationships, we work harder to invent options that are good for our partners and great for us. Often business partnerships are important to a company's strategy, but some are more important than others. This is especially true in supply chains, where producers of key components can be irreplaceable. When you are negotiating with such partners, you want to move into the trading zone as quickly as possible. But just because you are negotiating with a strategic partner doesn't mean you shouldn't try to claim as much value as you possibly can in such negotiations. By adjusting your approach when bargaining with a partner who is key to your strategy, you can build alliances in ways that will help you win at win-win negotiation.

Consider the relationship between "Brattlebury Corporation," which manufactures computers and peripherals, and "Viatex," the company that supplies the plastic ink cartridges for Brattlebury's printers. The companies' ten-year relationship has been a boon to both. For the past five years, the annual value of their contract has averaged $30 million.

But recently Brattlebury's overall sales have been flatter than expected. In addition, a survey revealed that many of Brattlebury's suppliers have grown dissatisfied with the company's periodic requests for proposals. Negotiating a proposal every two years was costing everyone time and money.

So Brattlebury's management resolved to explore cost-cutting measures with strategic partners like Viatex that provided crucial goods. These suppliers could not be replaced readily, and their goodwill was vital to meeting short-term corporate objectives.

Such relationships require special care and handling. During negotiations with a highly valued partner, negotiators must balance the need to get the lowest price possible with the need to maintain and enhance the alliance. Even if your company is not deeply embedded in a supply chain, you probably face ongoing negotiations with partners whose trust you want to preserve for strategic reasons. Here are five negotiating tactics that should become your standard practice when bargaining with a strategic partner. These will not block your way into the trading zone or minimize the chances of claiming a disproportionate share of the value you create.

Pay close attention to your partner's unique needs and interests. As I have already pointed out, to signal commitment to maintaining their long-term strategic relationship, negotiators need to listen carefully to one another's thoughts and feelings. Meeting regularly to probe interests is a simple but effective way to build relationships.

After identifying Viatex as a strategic partner, Brattlebury decided to present the supplier with the following proposal: a longer-term contract in exchange for 5 percent annual cost reductions. In addition, Brattlebury promised to collaborate on finding creative ways to make these cost cuts a reality, such as changing its specifications and requirements.

In meetings over the course of several months, representatives from Brattlebury and Viatex identified four potential ways to lower costs:

1. For the cartridges, Viatex could switch to a plastic that is considerably cheaper to source but that carries a slightly higher defect rate.
2. Currently, Viatex produces three designs for Brattlebury's various printer lines. Brattlebury could change its specifications so that Viatex would need to produce only one design.
3. Brattlebury could agree to minimum and maximum delivery quantities each quarter. This would prevent Viatex from having to lay off employees during slow periods and hire and train employees during peak times.
4. Viatex could save money by doing fewer quality control checks at its plant if Brattlebury were willing to take on more liability for product defects.

After identifying possible moves that would be beneficial to both partners, each side worked independently to assess its actual costs and the savings associated with each proposed change.

Keep in mind that everyone's interests always change in response to the unique opportunities and pressures they experience, both internal and external. Through regularly scheduled meetings, strategic partners can stay closely attuned to each other's shifting interests and explore unexpected yet mutually advantageous opportunities.

Focus more on creating value, less on distributional battles. While value creation is a cooperative enterprise, value distribution is primarily competitive—gains for one side typically generate losses for the other.

When negotiating with your most important strategic allies, emphasize creating value even more than you would with nonstrategic partners. This might mean devoting more time to brainstorming, considering more complex packages than usual, and sharing more details about your interests than you otherwise might. Winning at win-win negotiation with a strategic ally should be framed in terms of long-term gains and losses. With a long-term relationship comes an array of chances to recoup the value you may have forgone in one particular exchange.

By listening carefully to each other, Brattlebury and Viatex identified four possible ways to save money and add value. But how should they distribute the joint savings or gains they are creating between them? The answer depends on what is most important to each side. Remember that Brattlebury wants to achieve 5 percent savings from Viatex per year. Consequently, Brattlebury and Viatex must cut $1.5 million from this year's $30 million contract to protect the status of their strategic relationship.

Emphasize the relationship's long-term importance. When a business relationship is critical, we need to devote not only more time and energy to it but also more of ourselves. By getting to know your partners on a personal level, you can create social capital—goodwill or trust you can draw on over time. Something as simple as a business lunch—with time spent chatting about families or recent travel—can increase the chances that counterparts will believe each other when one insists that they have nothing more to offer on a particular issue.

Until individuals from Viatex and Brattlebury developed a strong working relationship over the course of numerous meetings and meals, anxiety about how to split potential joint gains stood in the way of realizing added benefits. A breakthrough moment came when a Viatex executive explained his concern about having to lay off employees and then later find qualified workers on short notice. In response, the Brattlebury executive suggested that Viatex take a more active role in ensuring that the $1.5 million cost-reduction target was met. Once they trusted each other enough to share their real priorities without fear of repercussions, the negotiators were able to improve their outcomes more than they originally thought possible.

Give strategic partners the benefit of the doubt. Cynicism runs rampant in today's business climate. When the representative of a strategic partner argues that she can't meet an important deadline or that she must have a higher price, you might be tempted to assume you're being manipulated. As a result, you dig in your heels, stiffening your resolve and rebuffing demands. Unfortunately, a suspicious first reaction can be self-fulfilling. If you think your negotiating partner is trying to gain leverage unfairly, you're likely to overreact, and the confrontation will escalate.

Instead, try giving strategic partners the benefit of the doubt when they make a special request. Take them at their word, then consider whether there's a way to solve their problem without harming your organization. When you show the other side that you're treating its requests seriously, you can avoid unnecessary rancor and preserve the relationship. You may not be able to find common ground, but you will certainly increase the odds of reaching a solution that pleases you both.

Let's consider the hidden agendas in the Viatex–Brattlebury negotiation. Viatex's executives are primarily concerned with protecting their workers so they can retain the skilled workforce required to produce their technical products. But if they can't achieve higher profits each year, they're prepared to walk away from the alliance with Brattlebury and seek other clients. Meanwhile, Brattlebury doesn't necessarily need a full 5 percent price cut from Viatex; it can actually save more than $1 million over the next five years simply by eliminating the administrative costs associated with the biannual RFP process.

Revealing these truths would require a great deal of trust on both sides. To identify the gains in the first place, each side must share some confidential information. Yet they both face pressure to keep this information under wraps, for fear the other side will get more than its fair share of the savings created. If Brattlebury thinks that Viatex might achieve greater benefits from the new agreement than Viatex has indicated, Brattlebury must be able to say so without destroying whatever trust has been built.

Avoid surprising partners you care about. No one likes surprises in a negotiation. We want to believe we've considered all the possibilities internally before coming to the negotiation table. Surprises reveal that we're unprepared, and they also expose us to risk.

One of the easiest ways to rupture a good working relationship is to surprise a strategic partner with an unexpected change in procedure or a nonnegotiable demand. Surprising someone by raising an issue for which he can't possibly be prepared is disrespectful, as is asking for a decision before he's had a chance to understand the risks involved. Catching someone off guard might cause him to err in your favor, but you'll pay the price later when he seeks retribution.

The challenge for strategic allies is to move effortlessly into value creation and only after that fall back on value distribution, with an emphasis on fairness and trust. By following this approach, negotiators can move quickly into the trading zone, where they can actually help each other maximize the value they take away from the deal.

Public-Private Strategic Partnerships

INSTEAD OF APPLYING the heavy hand of regulation, some U.S. government agencies are seeking to create public–private partnerships that offer incentives and support to corporations and nonprofit organizations willing to go beyond federal performance standards. In the context of civic redevelopment, for example, environmental agencies have offered developers of brownfields—contaminated, abandoned plots of land—extra latitude in terms of site cleanups, as well as relaxation of zoning limitations, as long as the developers are willing to work with relevant neighborhood organizations and give them the technical and financial support they need to participate. In addition, federal funds are granted commensurate with actual community improvements. Such public–private partnerships, which resemble strategic alliances in the supply chain, should be approached with the same principles in mind.

WHEN THE OTHER SIDE IS A KEY STRATEGIC PARTNER:

- *Know their needs and interests*
- *Create as much value as you can*
- *Emphasize the value of your long-term relationship*
- *Give them the benefit of the doubt*
- *Avoid surprising them*

Winning at win-win negotiation with strategic partners requires a light touch. When long-term relationships between companies or negotiating partners are important, how much you win in the short term (in a single deal) is less important than maintaining relationships and leaving open the possibility of doing especially well in future interactions.

Now we'll move from interactions between separate companies, albeit with long-term relationships, to internal negotiations within a single company. Getting into the trading zone can be just as difficult here, and the difficulties surrounding creating and claiming of value, just as tricky.

MANAGING CONFLICT WITHIN THE RANKS

THE SALES FORCE of a major investment firm, "Wall Street Associates," sold its financial products on a nationwide basis and reported to national product managers responsible for calculating their annual bonuses. When Wall Street Associates went through a restructuring, it upended this long-standing internal relationship. The salespeople were told they would also be reporting to new regional account managers, who would have a say about their bonuses as well. Around the same time, the national managers revealed that they wanted to alter how the sales force allocated its time and efforts.

The sales staff was up in arms. How could they divide their attention between the demands of two sets of managers at the same organizational level—a matrix management approach? The sense that their loyalties had been split led to a sales staff rebellion. Several superstar staff members threatened to quit.

Many companies have become pressure cookers of late. Internal conflicts boil over when top management imposes broad changes in business practices—demanding a switch to a new companywide computer system, for example, or redrawing lines of authority, as in the case of the restructuring faced by the sales force of Wall Street Associates. Conflicts between coworkers and between divisions waste resources, undermine effectiveness, and distract everyone from their goals.

Internal conflict has become a virtual epidemic in organizations for several reasons:

- Organizations are flatter and more networked than ever before. Many managers find themselves trying to meet responsibilities that extend beyond their authority—a primary cause of internal tension.
- Organizations must adapt to rapidly shifting environmental constraints, such as changing legal and regulatory requirements. Efforts to promote such adjustments often trigger obstructionist behavior.

- Organizations are working to increase diversity, a beneficial change that's nonetheless often accompanied by individual clashes in culture and style.
- As organizations face mounting pressure to "do more with less," internal departments often find themselves competing for scarce resources.

The best way to work out these internal conflicts is through direct negotiations among those affected by proposed management changes. Efforts to impose solutions from the top, although still the norm, are not as effective as agreements reached voluntarily by those who know the most about whatever has to be worked out and by those who have to implement new ways of doing business. Even though we are talking about parties who are members of the same organization, these negotiations are no less contentious that those involving parties from separate companies.

Conventional wisdom places primary responsibility for resolving internal conflict in the hands of top management. According to the prevailing view, senior managers should insist that employees put aside personal differences for the good of the organization. Managers should strive to clarify roles and responsibilities because, presumably, conflict results from confusion about lines of authority or from turf overlap. If conflict persists, it's up to senior managers to dictate appropriate behavior.

This approach may suppress internal conflict, but it won't deal with its underlying causes. In seeking the path of least resistance, the top-down approach fails to address the organizationwide concerns likely to lead to similar conflicts in the future. It makes much more sense for top management to facil-itate carefully structured problem-solving negotiations among those with a stake in whatever needs to be changed.

Rather than demanding compliance, new ways of working are more likely to succeed in flatter organizations if all relevant stakeholders engage in a three-step problem-solving negotia-tion process: diagnose sources of conflict, build consensus from differences, and sell agreements.

Diagnose Sources of Conflict

THE FIRST STEP, never easy, is getting all parties to agree on the scope and source of the difficulties created by proposed changes. In the case of Wall Street Associates, this was a delicate task because anxieties were running high. A negotiated approach to addressing internal conflicts begins with a formal conflict assessment, so the senior vice president for sales hired "Bill," an external consultant versed in the mutual-gains approach to negotiation, to assess the situation. Bill conducted private inter-views with the national product managers, the regional account managers, and the most experienced members of the sales staff. He then offered a preliminary assessment of the situation.

To ensure that all stakeholders found his assessment mean-ingful, Bill grounded his presentation in benchmarks, docu-menting the impacts of the new matrix management approach. Based on what he heard, he suggested that it ought to be possi-ble for everyone involved to benefit from the restructuring: na-tional product sales could be increased through regional sales, thereby increasing everyone's sales commissions. His reframing of the proposed management change was aimed at moving ev-eryone into the trading zone as quickly as possible.

Top management encouraged Bill to initiate a negotiation process aimed at resolving tensions between the national product managers and the regional account managers. To achieve support for this, Bill organized a one-day meeting at which top management confirmed that it was committed to finding a solution that met everyone's interests.

Based on his extensive one-on-one confidential assessment interviews, Bill produced a map of the conflict. This included a chart identifying the urgency of each stakeholder group's concerns. He also prepared a work plan that set ground rules to guide the problem-solving effort and expressed the need for additional fact-finding. By verifying the map's accuracy with the interviewees, Bill helped all parties understand the essence of the conflict.

It's important for stakeholder groups to choose members to represent them in any problem-solving negotiation. After reviewing the assessment, the three key groups—national product managers, regional account managers, and sales staff—met to clarify their interests and to identify three representatives from each group who would meet to try to work things out. Bill organized a preliminary meeting of these nine individuals. In this case, finding the trading zone required careful representation of all of the relevant interests.

Build Consensus from Differences

THE SECOND STEP in this internal problem-solving negotiation was to identify a package of trades that would help make the matrix management plan work for everyone. Bill facilitated three half-day meetings of the nine-member task force over a period of several weeks. The process began with Bill prompting the group representatives to rank their interests. Some were tempted to present positions rather than interests. When this happened, he pressed them to explain the thinking behind their positions.

Once all groups had clarified their interests, they worked to develop ways of meeting one another's interests. How could the sales staff respond to their national product managers and to their regional account managers at the same time? What communication and coordination tools might help the sales staff achieve their quarterly targets? At one point, a factual disagreement regarding the sales force's employment contracts emerged. The group designated a subcommittee to investigate the matter and report back with answers. Such joint fact-finding enhances the likelihood that all stakeholders will trust the information collected. Thus, value creation in internal negotiations depends on joint fact-finding as much as it does in negotiations involving independent organizations.

Ultimately the group pulled together a package of suggestions. Each group representative offered justifications for the packages he or she liked the best, explaining how modifications in the proposed matrix management plan would meet the interests of their group *and* produce the best possible result for the company as a whole.

At the center of the task force's agreement were recommended changes for the reporting structure and new guidelines for allocating sales-force time to national and regional accounts. The salespeople had rebelled primarily because the new matrix management approach made it extremely unclear how each of them could match or beat previous commissions. The task force recommended that each salesperson negotiate a single annual sales contract signed by the two managers to whom the salesperson reported. It also proposed an appeals process for salespeople who felt their performance had not been properly assessed at bonus time.

All but one of the nine participants signed the proposal, which was then forwarded to the senior vice president for sales.

Throughout this process, Bill played a crucial role. Without neutral assistance, it's unlikely that a task force made up of disputing factions would have reached the trading zone quite so quickly. The consultant kept the members of the group on task, prodded them to come to meetings prepared, and urged them to stay in touch with their constituents. As the voice of reason, he helped keep individual members from skirting the process in an effort to advance their own interests. Finally, he agreed to lead the follow-up activities spelled out in the agreement.

Each faction was seeking to win, that is, to reshape the proposed matrix management plan in a way that would help them earn the greatest amount of money possible. Once Bill got them into the trading zone, they were able to discern a deal space in which no one would be worse off and everyone had a chance of generating higher commissions than they received in the past.

Sell Agreements and Overcome Resistance

THE TASK FORCE had reached an agreement, but their work wasn't finished. They still needed to cultivate support, frame the agreement strategically, and build a coalition to ensure implementation. As my colleague Deborah Kolb points out, all problem-solving negotiations inside a single organization must accomplish these three objectives.

First, cultivate support. Task force members can cultivate support for their agreement through "appreciative moves"— conversations that acknowledge the concerns of others. Along these lines, the task force members and the consultant, Bill, invested a great deal of time in one-on-one meetings with people who were not directly involved in the conflict but who might have had questions about what the group was proposing. The representatives came prepared with face-saving suggestions for those who might have been opposed to specific elements of the agreement. For example, task force members assured those opposed that they'd publicly receive credit for their role in instituting change. The way for one group to "win" at these negotiations was to be certain that other segments of the company had opportunities to increase their commissions as well.

Second, frame agreements strategically. To keep ideas on the agenda in the face of opposition, use "process moves"—interventions aimed at shaping positive perceptions, such as publicity for small victories. Again and again in meetings with organizational members, the task force emphasized that contending groups within the company were working together to solve the problem. Their goal: to make it clear that everyone would benefit if the task force's work caused quarterly sales to rebound.

Build a coalition to support change. Task forces such as this one can build a supporting coalition by making "power moves" that capitalize on the resources and agenda-setting powers of those in leadership positions. The task force was able to win over a number of high-level fence sitters by arguing that negotiated problem-solving, if successful, might well be used to solve other unresolved internal conflicts. As supporters of the

task force report made themselves known, blockers were iso-
lated, and a winning coalition emerged. Top management was
delighted to move forward in the way the task force suggested.

As the example of Wall Street Associates illustrates, internal conflict should be addressed not as a short-term problem but
rather as an opportunity for an organization to get better at resolving conflicts so that future management changes that might
generate opposition are easier to deal with. Winning at win-win
negotiation in internal situations requires the same commitment
to getting into the trading zone, and creating and then claiming
value, as winning in negotiations with external partners.

WHEN YOU SHOULDN'T GO IT ALONE

I'VE FOUND THAT when organizations carefully hand-pick
agents to represent them in new or difficult negotiations, and
give them appropriate instructions, these skilled individuals can
almost always lead their organization into the trading zone and
help it win at win-win negotiation. Agents are often in the best
possible position to create value since they can take a less competitive stand toward the other side, at least at the outset of a
negotiation.

"Prometheus," an American manufacturer of medical
equipment that recently completed its fifth year in business, had
just secured a patent on its primary product, a heart monitor
that looked like a significant advance in the state of the art. The
potential market, in fact, is even stronger than the company
had imagined, but there is a problem: its second round of venture capital funding is coming to an end. A few other manufac-
turers are about to go public with competitive products, albeit

ones that have not tested as well as the Prometheus product. To shore up funding for the big launch of its latest product in an entirely new market, Janice, the CEO, decided to explore joint venture possibilities with several overseas partners.

There is another problem, though. Janice has never been involved in joint venture negotiations before; what's more, she has never done business with an overseas investor. Also, it turns out that one of the European companies she approached knew all about her company's internal strengths and weaknesses, including its lack of overseas experience. Janice knows she is the one in the best position to represent her small company's interests in the upcoming negotiations, but she is extremely nervous. The company's future is on the line. Does she have enough knowledge and experience to succeed?

When you're approaching a new kind of negotiation, you need to be able to recognize when you're in over your head. In such cases, it might be smart to quit before you even begin. That is, it may make sense to have someone more experienced take your place at the table—an agent. There are circumstances in which agents will probably get better results than negotiators could ever hope to achieve on their own. To compensate for her lack of experience, Janice could bring in an agent to make contact with overseas investors, explore their interests, help her and her team examine their own interests, generate the terms of possible partnerships, assist in evaluating offers, and even close the deal. By hiring an agent as her adviser or stand-in, Janice could vastly improve her chances of concluding a successful joint venture. The mandate she should give the agent is to devote as much time and energy as possible to creating value.

If Janice's potential partners balk at dealing with her representative, she might involve the agent only at key moments. If, on the other hand, the partners bring their own agents onboard, the agents might converse among themselves, negotiating possible packages in consultation with their principals.

Some experts suggest that agents can prevent negotiators from discovering the trading zone—from making the transition from adversaries to cooperative problem solvers. According to this logic, an agent may have personal interests that clash with those of his principal, and this could keep negotiators from finding common ground. Yet I've found that when negotiators give appropriate instructions, their carefully chosen agents can almost always generate mutually advantageous deals.

When to Use Agents

THERE ARE THREE CIRCUMSTANCES in which you'll be better off tapping an agent to take your place at the bargaining table (at least for part of the negotiation process). This is especially true in the early stages, when value creation is easiest.

You're unfamiliar with the issues and rules at hand. Sometimes negotiations lead you out of your comfort zone and into unfamiliar territory. When you're unsure of the issues under discussion or the rules of the game, you'd be wise to seek an experienced agent. For instance, a scientist interested in securing support from investors for a new start-up would benefit from having a skilled lawyer or IPO specialist represent him. Similarly, someone who has never sold a house might prefer to have a real estate agent negotiate with prospective bidders and generate mutually advantageous trades. If the agent makes clear that he or she needs to check back with their principal before a deal can be closed, it sometimes creates more room for value-creating discussions.

Time or distance prevents you from doing your best. What if you're due to begin talks with someone in a distant city or country, or under a tight deadline to hammer out a deal? When you don't have the time to meet with potential partners in a distant location or participate in every step in the process, you're unlikely to represent yourself well. Also, you might be tempted to close too quickly. In such cases, you'll probably want to find an agent who specializes in the type of negotiation at stake. A California writer who has never dealt with commercial publishers, for example, should probably enlist a New York–based literary agent to sell her manuscript and explore contract terms.

You have a poor relationship with your negotiating partner. Imagine you're facing—and dreading—negotiations with someone you've clashed with in the past. By bringing in an agent, you can calm tempers and better ensure that talks are businesslike and amicable. This strategy plays out most dramatically in contentious diplomatic contexts, such as the negotiation of a cease-fire between armies, when factions might bring in representatives they both trust to hash out a peace agreement. In the business world, when rancor between a company and its employees over a work contract is deep-seated and ongoing, both sides may need to employ experienced agents to explore very different terms from those that applied in the past.

In short, whenever you're worried that you won't be able to pursue your interests effectively—especially in the face of aggressive behavior on the other side—you'd be well advised to find an agent to represent you.

Using Agents Effectively

ONCE YOU'VE DECIDED to use an agent, it's important not to rush headlong into the process—picking the first one you speak to, for example, and sending him off to talks the next day. You need to choose your agent carefully, and then establish a clear, detailed understanding of responsibilities and expectations. The following are critical steps in picking an agent and negotiating his contract.

Examine your potential agent's reputation closely. When choosing an agent, put your needs first. Agents specialize in different fields and have known reputations—differences that can improve or diminish your chances of getting the outcome you desire. You might choose a particular agent because of her previous success negotiating with principals in situations like yours. Or the choice could be based on the strong working relationship she has with people you know. Analyze agents' reputations from many angles while factoring in the particulars of your upcoming negotiation.

Clearly communicate your agent's responsibilities. After you've made your choice, it's time to write out the responsibilities you do and don't want her to handle. Start by ranking your interests and sharing this list with your agent. A professional athlete might put performance incentives at the top of his list as his agent prepares to negotiate the player's new contract. If the player's performance has declined recently, he might feel uncomfortable asking team owners for such upside benefits on his own. The player should also specify the degree of authority the agent will and won't have at various stages in the negotiation process. The agent might have a great deal of latitude early on but need verbal authorization from the player as the deal solidifies.

Negotiators often wonder whether they should give their agents broad or narrow parameters in which to settle. In my view, allowing your agent to explore a broad range of alternatives makes sense, especially during value creation, as long as she does not have the authority to make final commitments—which should always be yours to make. In other words, let your agent probe the edges of the deal space and report back to you. Together, think through possible trades that might create value on your behalf. Make sure any final deal has your approval before it is formalized.

Link agent compensation to performance. As the principal, you may want to include a provision in your agent's contract that ties her compensation to the achievement of certain negotiation milestones or results. In any circumstance, it is crucial for you to ensure that your agent's interests are tightly aligned with your own. This might mean holding your agent responsible not only for the dollar value of the deal but also for the quality of the working relationship between you and the other side in the wake of the negotiation.

In some negotiations, you may want to involve an agent just to bring fresh eyes to the situation. This may mean that an agent's involvement is most valuable during your own preparations and the initial value-creating brainstorming session with the other side. Keep in mind that when it comes time to accept or reject an offer, negotiators often defer too readily to their agents. If you want your agent to disengage at some point in the process, express that caveat clearly at the outset. Include it in the contract.

Working with Your Agent—and Someone Else's

NEGOTIATIONS BECOME ESPECIALLY COMPLEX when agents are involved on two or more sides. Many negotiators often mistakenly assume that an agent representing the other side always has a clear mandate from his principal, and always aligns his interests with those of the principal. Janice needs to be very careful about this in the Prometheus case because often, neither is true. For example, the agent on the other side may have been told by his principal that he will get a bonus only if he gets Janice to accept an unfavorable contract. He may have been given no other instructions. This means that her good ideas about ways to create additional value for both sides could well be ignored by the agent. Prometheus could actually lose money because the other side's agent had too narrow a mandate. For this reason, Janice should be aware of potential pitfalls and follow these general guidelines.

Explore the role of the other side's agent. Janice may suspect that the interests of the other party's agent are not aligned with those of his principal, but how can she find out for sure? She should consider speaking to the principal on the other side and probing to determine, to the extent possible, what he expects from his agent. If he won't cooperate, she should try writing down her understanding of his agent's interests and sending it directly to him (not to the agent) for confirmation. By doing so, she may be able to discover the nature of his relationship with his agent and the type of bargaining she can expect. An agent paid a percentage of whatever deal he generates may be in a rush to close because he needs the cash. Meanwhile, his principal might actually prefer to seek other tradeoffs that could enhance the deal and create value for both sides.

Make the other party's agent your ally. Whenever possible, frame proposals that will provoke the other side's agent to advocate your interests with his client (as discussed in chapter 1 and further in chapter 4). After all, if you aren't able to speak directly with the agent's client, the agent is the only person who can argue on your behalf. It's in your interest to arm the agent with the strongest case you can muster in support of your desired outcome. In addition, you should seek ways to meet the interests of both the agent and his principal. Make it easy for the agent to explain why your proposals should be accepted. A basic understanding of the agent's contract could be useful, though this information may be difficult to verify.

Put forward a variety of agreements. If the other side's agent is not interested in expanding the deal space, Janice will need to work at pulling them into the trading zone and generating proposals that are good for them (and great for her). She shouldn't hesitate to put multiple written proposals or packages on the table (making sure she can live with all of them). In doing so, she'll force the agent to discuss the choices she's offered with his principal.

Once you and the other party have reached agreement through your agents, remind your own agent that the final decision is yours to make. This power will not minimize your agent's ability to create value or generate a winning package for you, although your agent might argue otherwise in the hope of gaining more authority.

Finally, when it comes time to seal a deal, don't hesitate to insist upon a face-to-face meeting with the other side, with your agent present, even if she has been handling most of the contact up until that time.

Although professional agents can complicate negotiations, their presence is likely to enhance the ability of negotiators in unfamiliar territory to reach the trading zone and to generate winning packages. The key is to remember that agents on both sides always have interests that vary to some degree from those of their principals.

CHOOSE AN AGENT WHEN:

- *You're unfamiliar with the issues and rules*
- *Time or distance creates a barrier*
- *Poor relationships might get in the way*

USE AGENTS EFFECTIVELY BY:

- *Examining your potential agent's reputation*
- *Communicating responsibilities*
- *Linking compensation to performance*
- *Exploring the role of the other side's agent*
- *Making the other side's agent your ally and reviewing his or her responsibilities and powers*
- *Putting forth a variety of possible agreements*

By carefully crafting a written agreement with her own agent and staying attuned to the agenda of the other party's agent, Janice should be able to generate the kind of agreement that allows her to claim her fair share of the joint venture.

WHEN A MAJORITY ISN'T ENOUGH

CONSIDER HOW A TYPICAL WORK GROUP inside a company or organization reaches decisions. A leader sets the group's objectives, mandates a schedule, and indicates who will be at the table (often with the concurrence of others). When the discussions are complete, the work group takes a straw poll or a vote of some kind. In most instances, the majority rules, although someone higher up may eventually supersede the group's authority. This is not an ideal context in which to push value creation as far as it can go.

While most work groups don't follow all the requirements of Robert's Rules of Order, they do tend to adopt, most of the time, at least two key features of parliamentary procedure: they employ a system by which (1) motions are made and informally seconded, and (2) final decisions are made by a majority. Such procedures don't always maximize the chances of value creation. If top management knew what it wanted the outcome to be, it probably wouldn't bother creating the work group. So the work group should do everything it can to explore value-creating opportunities. This often requires alternative decision-making procedures.

Why do work groups and teams rely on voting or majority rule as their primary means of making decisions, especially when voting shuts down the search for creative outcomes? First, because they think it prevents the few from dictating to the many, thereby establishing a sense of fairness. Second, it leads to a firm decision. When deadlines loom, a vote effectively ends discussion. Finally, majority rule presumably enhances the legitimacy of whatever decision or recommendation emerges by communicating to others that more people liked the proposal than didn't.

There's one big problem with majority rule, however: it puts a premium on generating just enough support to put a majority together rather than on producing the best possible outcome, that is, producing as much value as possible for everyone. As a consequence, majority-rule decisions almost always guarantee an unhappy minority—and, therefore, some degree of instability. I know one multinational company, call them "Simplex," that spent a year debating which division's accounting software would become the system of choice for the whole company. The members of the eight-person work group spent almost a year advocating for their division's software, convinced that the winner would be able to devote a lot less time to making adjustments. The oldest division was persuasive, and, by majority vote, imposed its will. An unhappy minority set out to show that this was a bad decision, awaiting an opportunity to sabotage or reverse the group's choice. In a group decision-making situation, I would argue, it is important to find a way to reach decisions that help as many parties as possible to meet their most important concerns. Often, this means working harder to create even more value to bring the holdouts on board.

A Better Way

MOST PEOPLE HAVE A VAGUE SENSE that some kind of consensus-building process would be better than a simple majority. It would certainly avoid the tyranny of the majority and increase the legitimacy of work group decisions.

Consensus building involves moving almost all the members of a group simultaneously into the trading zone. It requires a commitment to seek overwhelming agreement among all relevant stakeholders. The result is a negotiated decision that is as close to unanimous as possible. From an organizational standpoint, it means helping the group as a whole win. More than just human relations jargon for getting everyone to cooperate, consensus building allows a group to reach the broadest agreement possible, not just one that is barely acceptable to a majority. I will walk through a consensus-building process and show how it can improve group decision making in your organization. If you want to help your organization win at win-win negotiation, it helps to advocate for a consensus-building rather than a majority rule approach to group decision making. Even in situations where you think you can be part of a winning majority, remember that an unhappy minority may devote substantial time and energy to upending a decision that didn't meet its needs, as in the above-mentioned Simplex case.

Consensus Building: A Five-Step Process

CONSIDER THE FOLLOWING SITUATION. In an effort to adjust to new federal legislation, a small health services company called "Best Care" realizes that it must make a number of changes to the way it operates, especially in terms of the way it hires and compensates part-time consultants. The CEO, the general counsel, the CFO, and the HR director are well aware of what must be accomplished in a matter of months. They have appointed a task force with a half-dozen members to figure out exactly how to bring Best Care into compliance with the new laws and emerging regulations. The task force includes key individuals with the most knowledge and experience from finance, legal, human resources, sales, and marketing. Each task force member has clear instructions from their immediate supervisor to make sure that any proposed changes are acceptable from their supervisor's standpoint. The first few meetings have made clear that there are very different ideas about what needs to be accomplished, by when, at what costs, using which strategies. Reaching consensus may prove difficult also because most of the task force members are unhappy with the CEO's decision to appoint Brad, assistant general counsel, as head of the task force.

Let's look at the five steps in the consensus-building process as they were applied in this group.

1. Convene the group. The CEO is the convener. It is his job to define what needs to be done, indicate who needs to be at the table, and provide the resources necessary for the group to engage in a problem-solving dialogue.

In consensus building, the convener often taps a neutral facilitator—someone from inside the organization—to canvas possible stakeholders and lead the discussion. In this case, the CEO has appointed Brad to head the team. Brad is certainly not neutral. He has been appointed to ensure that the job gets done. On the other hand, figuring out what Best Care needs to do means taking account of the multiple ways the new law and forthcoming regulations will affect each aspect of the company's operations. It will require substantial insight into the technical workings of each component of the organization. And it will require buy-in from everyone if a seamless transition is to occur.

Brad reports to the general counsel that the group has already made it clear that they have no intention of deferring to the legal department in figuring out what needs to be done. The general counsel suggests to Brad that they hire a trained facilitator to interview, privately and confidentially, not just the members of the task force but an additional dozen or so individuals who might be able to spell out how the company's reliance on part-time consultants is likely to run afoul of the new law and regulations. If they have to hire full-time employees to do the same work, there will be all kinds of financial and logistical implications. Based on the interviews, which the facilitator completes in a few weeks, she produces a written analysis summarizing possible ways to comply with the new law, along with arguments for and against each suggestion. Everyone interviewed receives a copy of the facilitator's report. After producing a revised draft, taking account of confidential feedback she received, the facilitator helps Brad spell out a specific agenda, timetable, ground rules, and two possible additions to the original team. The CEO quickly embraces the facilitator's suggestions.

2. Clarify responsibilities. At this point it's important to clarify who will assume which responsibilities within the task force. While Brad is clearly in charge, he might prefer to have the facilitator manage group meetings.

Here's where consensus building differs markedly from the typical majority rule approach. The only way to get a near-unanimous outcome is to make sure that everyone involved understands that they are responsible for formulating proposals that meet not only their own needs but the needs of everyone else at the table as well. Why? If all you need is a majority, you're likely to spend time outside the meeting piecing together a winning coalition. Once you have it, you won't care much about what those outside the coalition have to say. But if you don't take account of the concerns of a losing minority, your victory may be short-lived. Thus, the goal is to organize a problem-solving process that aims to produce a result that each team member will say is good for everyone else, good for Best Care, and great for them.

In a consensus-building process, everyone understands that they won't be able to achieve their own goals unless they help others achieve theirs. Now the group's face-to-face work requires creating as much value as possible, making sure the results meet Best Care's overall interests (as defined by the CEO and others in senior management), and ensuring that a win for any one part of the company represents more than a minimally acceptable result for the others.

The person leading the meetings, whether it's Brad or the facilitator, must be proficient in group problem-solving techniques. A recorder should be assigned to produce ongoing summaries of key points of agreement so that there is one ongoing narrative describing the task force's efforts. And team members must agree to an explicit set of ground rules governing their interactions.

In the case of Best Care, the facilitator suggested ground rules that included statements such as, "The group will seek unanimity, but it will settle for overwhelming agreement after every possible effort has been made to meet the concerns of everyone involved."

3. Deliberate and brainstorm. In consensus building it's important for team members to debate issues in a way that draws upon the best joint fact-finding information available and upon a broad range of possible ways to respond to everyone's concerns. The goal of consensus-building deliberations can be understood as maximizing joint gains—coming as close as possible to meeting all the underlying interests of the relevant stakehold-ers. By brainstorming value-creating options, the team increases the chances that it will reach an informed consensus. Again, this agreement is the key to everyone achieving an outcome that is better for Best Care and better for each department than no agreement. It is within this context that each party must de-cide how to handle the difficult aspects of value claiming.

In its first few meetings, the Best Care team brainstorms ways of tackling the part-time consultant problem. Each mem-ber of the task force explains why the current situation works for them. Switching from part-time consultants (who can be easily added or let go as service demands shift geographically or re-quired specialties change) to full-time employees on fixed salaries will have financial, legal, hiring, and operational ramifications. Additional managers may need to be hired. Training will be-come a more expensive line item. Reporting lines will need to be shifted. Depending on how these changes are implemented, marketing and sales may have to repackage what they are selling.

The department that has to make the fewest or least dis-ruptive changes thinks it will win. But the best interests of the company and the best interests of the other departments may require substantial changes across the board. Reallocating re-sources (or rewards) to departments that have to make the most substantial shifts could change everyone's calculations. Instead of defining success as minimizing the need to change, a very different framing that opens up new and desirable opportu-nities for each department could mean that each department imagines a very different winning outcome.

4. Reach a decision. In a consensus-building process, reach-ing a decision isn't as simple as taking a vote. Rather, it means continually adding to a package of recommendations aimed at meeting everyone's interests. The goal is unanimity, but overwhelming agreement is sufficient. Your desire, of course, if unanimity is not possible, is to be part of the "winning" group.

The group's leader manages the decision-making process by summarizing each proposed package. "Who can't live with this?" she will ask. If anyone indicates opposition, that person has the burden of suggesting ways to make the package acceptable to them—without making it worse for anyone else.

Eventually, the facilitator produces a final report for which the group leader feels comfortable taking responsibility. Group members are asked to take the proposed package of recommendations back to their department for comment. In their final report to the CEO, the team may propose radical changes in the way various departments operate, particularly during the transition.

At the final scheduled meeting, Brad or the facilitator asks team members whether they can live with the package they have taken back to their department for review. Last-minute improvements address almost all outstanding issues. When no one can come up with some other way to create additional value, the group thinks its work is done. But the representative of one department, unable to get the draft report to accommodate its existing practices while still incorporating everyone else's concerns and suggestions, refuses to sign. The others, however, do sign the final recommendations, noting their commitment to work to implement them.

Brad then delivers the task force report to the CEO, indicating that consensus (but not unanimity) has been reached. The document describes the concerns of the department that was unable to support the package. Those who are part of the agreement consider themselves victorious.

5. Implement the decision. The group's work isn't actually done. Consensus building extends through implementation. The team needs to keep in touch regularly so that they can iron out any kinks that emerge.

Suppose that problems arise as Best Care lays off a number of experienced consultants while trying to hire new full-time staff. Rather than abandoning the new procedures, Brad might reconvene the task force to brainstorm ways of dealing with these problems. The task force is the ideal group to monitor implementation and tweak new procedures once they've been put in place.

Consensus Building Produces Better Results

CONSENSUS BUILDING TAPS the knowledge and skill of everyone in a group. It doesn't depend on the strength of the leader or a bare majority to push through a winning agreement. It allows for a neutral facilitator—someone who has no interest in pushing his or her own agenda—to manage problem-solving conversations. And it gives everyone an incentive to keep searching for ways to create value when the going gets tough, since there won't be any agreement until almost everyone gets on board.

The standard practice in work groups is to settle for what a majority wants or, worse still, to defer to a solution imposed from the top. Consensus building is the best alternative when a majority is not enough to ensure legitimacy and effective implementation. When cast in a leadership role, people like Brad focus almost entirely on getting the job done—rather than on doing the best possible job. Many leaders are more interested in taming their group than in tapping the group's full creative potential.

INSTEAD OF MAKING DECISIONS BY
MAJORITY RULE, BUILD CONSENSUS:

- *Convene the group*
- *Clarify responsibilities*
- *Deliberate and brainstorm*
- *Reach a decision*
- *Implement the decision*

Because group members must learn how to operate in a new way, the transition process from a majority rule orientation to consensus building can be slow. Organizations may need to invest in building their facilitation capabilities, either by training employees or hiring outsiders. In the long term, these costs pay off in the form of better decisions as well as employees, customers, and constituents who are more satisfied. Winning at win-win negotiation requires a commitment to consensus building.

3

EXPECT THE UNEXPECTED

*Use Contingent Offers to Claim More
Than the Other Side*

THE ART OF THE IMPROVISER

WHETHER SEATED AT THE PIANO or at the bargaining table, expect the unexpected. The best negotiators know how to turn
moments of surprise into opportunities to create something of
value and significance. Just as jazz musicians spend long hours
learning to be spontaneous, negotiators will have more opportunities to get into the trading zone and claim more than the
other side if they enhance their improvisational skills.

At the Program on Negotiation at Harvard Law School,
we've engaged in an ongoing study of improvisation in fields
such as music, theater, and psychoanalysis. Two of my colleagues, Lakshmi Balachandra and Michael Wheeler, suggest
several lessons that negotiators can use once they are in the
trading zone. Overall, our work to date suggests that business
negotiators would benefit from building a repertoire of improvisational capabilities, including attentiveness, flexibility, and a
willingness to take advantage of the element of surprise. Later
in this chapter I will talk about contingent agreements that can

be used to deal with surprises that you think are coming but you can't predict with any accuracy.

Successful Improvisers Are Attentive

FOR AN IMPROVISED JAZZ PIECE to really swing, each member of the band must be fully attuned not only to the chord changes and tempo but also to the attitude of the other performers. If one musician shifts to a minor key during a solo, the others quickly adjust to the new mood. Along these lines, a cardinal rule of improv comedy is to unconditionally accept the "offers" contained in the statements of other performers.

Similarly, in a business negotiation, no matter what assumptions you bring to your first session, you have to listen closely to discern whether your counterpart is behaving as you expected. For example, imagine that your investment company hopes to purchase a commercial property you've targeted in a major urban center. In informal conversation, one of the property owners encourages you to make an offer to buy. You set up a meeting with his rep and prepare extensively for what you assume will be a typical real estate negotiation, determining the property's market value, assessing the likely development trends, and testing your company's willingness to pay.

Once the initial pleasantries of your long-anticipated meeting wind down, you inquire about the asking price. The smile disappears from your counterpart's face. Her answer takes you by surprise: "It's not for sale."

Thrown off guard, you wonder if she's playing hardball. Or is she so uncertain of her property's worth that she's afraid to toss out the first offer and anchor too low? With your homework to back you up, you make a preemptive offer that's well below the amount your firm is actually willing to pay.

"As I just said, the property is not for sale," she repeats.

"Come on," you say, puzzled and annoyed. "Joe told me you were interested in selling. You must have a number in mind."

"No," she replies tensely. "Actually, I don't."

Her discomfort and reserve suggest something other than outright rejection. Should you get up and leave, raise your bid, or probe further? You take the third track: "Suppose we were business partners in this venture. What are your long-term plans for this property? Maybe there's a way we could help you achieve your objectives."

The rep's posture changes immediately. She relaxes. She smiles. Then she says, "The truth is, we've decided there's a huge upside for redevelopment. It seems that one of the adjacent parcels is going to be developed as a hotel, so we've decided to hold on to the property for a while."

Based on your reading of both her verbal and nonverbal cues, you continue to improvise. "What if we became partners? We could help you put together a redevelopment plan. I haven't talked with my partners about this, but we might be able to bring significant financing to the table."

Standard negotiation theory stresses the need to brainstorm value-creating tradeoffs. The study of improvisation adds another step: to create value, don't just think outside the box; remain attentive to the mood, posture, and unspoken signals your counterpart offers. Improvise questions aimed at maximizing value and opportunities for both of you, then listen carefully to how the other side responds. Winning in this situation means listening for entirely new opportunities. Practice being more fully attentive. At every moment in a negotiation, your counterpart is sending unspoken messages. If your substantive preparation is sufficient and your general confidence level high enough, you can devote more of your attention to picking up these important signals

Successful Improvisers Are Flexible

YOU'VE FOCUSED ON reading your counterpart's intentions and asked questions that probe her interests. The next step in successful negotiation improvisation is to put aside your predetermined strategies and tactics and invent new ones on the spot. The ability to make impromptu adjustments requires flexibility. Just like musicians and other performers, some negotiators are endlessly and effortlessly flexible, while others need to become more comfortable with unplanned explorations.

One example from a negotiation I was involved in concerned "Painkillers," a pharmaceutical company that for many years supplied a Veterans' Administration (VA) hospital pharmacy with one of the most effective (and expensive) drugs for the treatment of prostate cancer. The company's exclusive patent had expired, however, and generic versions of the drug were about to hit the market. Seeking to maintain its market share, the drug company's sales team determined that they might be able to keep their customers for at least another year by raising doubts about the efficacy of the generic version of the drug.

Here's a snippet of the type of dialogue that occurred between the head of the VA pharmacy and the drug company's sales rep.

Pharmacy head: We don't see a reason to pay any more than the going rate for the generic version.

Sales rep: Be careful. You can't be certain that the generic will be fully effective. Do you really want to take that risk?

Pharmacy head: What are you suggesting?

Sales rep: We could reduce the current price we charge you by 50 percent if you commit to buying 100 percent of your supply from us for at least the next three years.

Pharmacy head: I don't think I can do that. That would still be almost twice as much as the generic is going to cost.

Sales rep: Well, we could give you a 30 percent discount if you commit to two years.

Pharmacy head: You don't get it. My advisory board will be all over me if I don't supply the generic version at the lowest possible price.

It's become clear that the Painkillers rep needs to jettison her original strategy; offering a discount on the prevailing price in exchange for a multiyear commitment just isn't working. On the fly, she presents an entirely new plan.

Sales rep: What if we were to put together a package? You continue to buy our drug for the next three years at 50 percent off the current price, *and* we give you a 10 percent discount on all your other orders from us for the next calendar year.

Pharmacy head: Do you mean *all* of the other drugs we buy from you?

Sales rep: Yes. I have here a printout of everything you purchased from us last year. I'm offering a 10 percent discount on all these drugs for the coming year—in exchange for you sticking with our version of [Drug X] for three years at half price.

Pharmacy head: Well, that may give me what I need to convince my advisory committee that we should continue to buy the drug from you.

By considering the substantial volume of other drugs that the hospital was buying from her company, the sales rep was able to suggest an entirely new package. The key to her success: abandoning the sales team's carefully planned proposal and being willing to play the What-If Game.

Too many organizations demand that their negotiators get preapproval for their script, usually from the legal and financial departments. This policy hinders flexible exploration of better alternatives. So seek permission to explore new options on the spot. Lobby your superiors for the freedom to brainstorm innovative proposals at the bargaining table (without making any commitments); then, clear any proposed agreements back at the office. What-if proposals should clearly reflect preapproved parameters set during internal preparatory talks. And they should always be offered with the proviso that both sides will need to get final approval before any deal can be sealed.

Successful Improvisers Use the Element of Surprise

MANY BUSINESS NEGOTIATORS open talks by trying to out-intimidate each other. Consider this all-too-typical script between two potential business partners:

"There's no point continuing this conversation unless you concede that I deserve 90 percent of future earnings—my fair share, considering how much time and money I'm expending up front."

"Ninety for you and ten for me? Are you out of your mind? I won't settle for less than 60 percent."

And so the hard-bargaining ping-pong match begins.

But what if the second speaker had responded like this: "Ninety percent might be feasible, but I think there's a lot more value we can create before we reach any final decision. I have some ideas about how to turn our business into a real winner for both of us. I assume you agree that if I can show you how we can double or triple our earnings, then I ought to get the lion's share of the added value."

Most hard bargainers will be taken aback when you try to shift from a win-lose mindset to one of value creation and collaboration. That leaves the door open for the person who makes such a surprising move to do a bit of claiming for herself. Sometimes the most compelling surprises have little or nothing to do with the substance of the negotiation. Suppose you notice that your counterpart is in a foul mood, for example. Instead of responding to his unreasonable opening offer, you might inquire about his life away from the table. "You don't seem like yourself today, and I'm guessing this has little to do with our conversation," you might say. "Do you want to talk about what's troubling you?" He'll likely be suspicious of your motives at first, and there's no guarantee he'll open up about his difficulties. But by expressing genuine concern for his well-being, you should at least be able to clear the air.

The jazz improvisers we've interviewed (and observed) indicate that unexpected moves by one member of an ensemble often lead to the most interesting, exciting, and satisfying group outcomes. Similarly, when you try out a surprising move in a negotiation, as long as you do it in a tentative fashion, you are likely to nudge stalled talks in a productive direction.

Prior to the negotiation, contemplate a few surprise moves in advance. Role-play the responses you might get to an unexpected statement or question—and your subsequent reactions—with some of your colleagues. Planned surprises may appear to be a contradiction in terms, but skilled performers told us they always have a set of potential options and responses they can draw on during their act. They also said that successful improv requires an element of playfulness—a willingness to look silly, not take yourself too seriously, and try things you've never done before. Winning at win-win negotiation may require a willingness to depart from a set script and a lot more improvisation than most people expect. The value of this approach can be even better illustrated by situations involving conversations with "true believers," people who seem to stick to their beliefs no matter what evidence is presented. All too often the result is a shouting match in which little, if anything, is accomplished. It is entirely possible, on the other hand, to have productive conversations about a controversial issue, such as climate change, for example, without needing to agree on what is causing it.

TALKING TO CLIMATE CHANGE SKEPTICS

I HAD AN OPPORTUNITY to speak at Harvard University to a room packed with students and community residents seeking advice on how to talk to climate change skeptics. The students would soon be heading home for Thanksgiving and were looking for suggestions about how to talk to family and friends who either don't believe that global warming is happening or accept the fact that the climate is getting warmer but attribute relatively recent temperature changes to natural rather than human causes. To get things started, we heard from a local radio talk show host who really is a climate change skeptic. He made it very clear that he didn't trust Al Gore, was sure that scientists disagree about almost everything (because that's what science requires), and thought that anyone who believes that climate change is the result of human activity (rather than cyclical natural phenomena) has been sold a bill of goods.

First, I tried to make clear that seeking to convert "non-believers" is probably a mistake, and is certainly no way to encourage constructive dialogue. Rather, I suggested, the goal of dialogue ought to be to share ideas, advance the cause of mutual understanding, and see what opportunities to reach agreement might exist—in spite of fundamental differences in beliefs or levels of understanding. A number of the students at the meeting found this unacceptable. From their standpoint, the threat posed by the continued buildup of greenhouse gases in the atmosphere is so frightening that they feel compelled to convince anyone who doesn't believe this to admit that they are wrong. They want to repeat and review what the vast majority of atmospheric scientists know to be true: The atmosphere is warming. This is caused by the buildup of greenhouse gases, particularly CO_2 and methane. This build-up is caused by human activity, particularly the burning of fossil fuels. And the end result will be a worldwide catastrophe—rising sea levels that will inundate vast coastal areas, particularly in the developing world; increasing storm intensification that will cause destructive flooding and Katrina- and Sandy-like devastation; increased drought in some areas, and increasing numbers of extremely hot days that may cause massive eco-migration; more rapid spread of airborne disease; and irreversible harm to a range of marine and terrestrial species and habitats. The skeptic on the dais with me indicated that scientists can't possibly know exactly when and where such things will and won't happen (and he's right). He also insisted that even if warming is occurring, it is impossible to know for sure whether it is mostly or entirely caused by human activity or nothing more than a natural phenomenon.

That was my cue. I said I didn't think that mattered. I urged people interested in engaging in useful conversation with skeptics to shift their conversations to a discussion of risk—to talk about risk and risk management. I used the example of earthquakes. We don't need to know for sure whether (where and when) an earthquake will occur to seriously consider taking action to minimize the severe adverse effects an earthquake could cause if it does occur. It turns out, we can require construction standards in new buildings that will protect people from collapsing structures. We can even retrofit existing buildings to make them more earthquake-proof (although this comes at a cost). While there doesn't seem to be anything we can do to reduce the odds of an earthquake occurring, there are lots of things we can do (including organizing and practicing emergency evacuation efforts) to save lives and reduce misery and reconstruction costs when earthquakes do occur. Even if the majority of scientists are right—that if we don't reduce to 350–450 parts per million of CO_2 equivalents in the next fifty years, the worst effects of climate change will be impossible to correct—we won't be able to reduce greenhouse gas emissions enough over the next three decades to mitigate those effects. Given the chance that the many thousands of scientists around the world who study these issues might be right, we could look for things to do that will reduce the disastrous effects if climate change is, in fact, occurring. Also, if we could find things that simultaneously achieve other laudable objectives (that help almost everyone), why would anyone be opposed?

So I suggested reframing the discussion around what is called "adaptation." If we can switch to energy sources that don't involve the burning of fossil fuels, but instead rely on infinite energy sources like sunlight, wind, ocean waves, biofuels, and the flow of fresh water, we may be able to simultaneously reduce the adverse effects of climate change (if it does occur), decrease our country's dependence on imported oil and gas, dramatically reduce health dangers to human beings, minimize the ecological damage caused by air and water pollution and the degradation of surface lands, and create more jobs in our own country. This would be a "no-regrets" response to the possibility of climate change. Similarly, if we can help every household reduce the amount of electricity it wastes (especially at peak times), we can eliminate the need to build new power plants, thereby reducing everybody's electricity rates and saving all consumers money. Even if the risks are not fully predictable, a shift to renewable energy (especially if planned in a way that compensates anyone who suffers any losses in the short term as a result of the shift) would be a more desirable way to proceed. If you think about each component of climate change risk, it should be possible to brainstorm adaptive responses that minimize the chances of serious harm to the public and to the environment while simultaneously improving the economy and enhancing social well-being.

Conversations with climate change skeptics—in fact with any true believer—no matter what social or business issue is involved, require improvisation. When someone expresses strong opposition to prevailing scientific findings, don't challenge them (or call them names!). Instead, ask them to join you in a thought experiment that fits the situation. For example, ask them a thoughtful question and then follow up with some brainstorm ideas:

- Whatever you think the chances are that a buildup of greenhouse gases in the atmosphere is causing global temperatures to rise, and that such increases will trigger a host of dangerous and costly consequences, can we brainstorm cost-effective ways to reduce the harm that would occur if the worst happens and achieve a host of other benefits at the same time?

- Improved emergency preparedness in cities will help if flooding of the sort that occurred in New Orleans and the New York–New Jersey area happens more often. (Increased storm intensity is one of the anticipated effects of climate change.) It will also help cities respond to any kind of natural or human-made emergency. Almost every city could do more at a modest cost to update and practice its emergency response procedures.

- Investments in expensive transportation, wastewater treatment, and other municipal infrastructure should probably be made with greater consideration of the possibility of rising sea levels, saltwater intrusion into freshwater marshes, and increased storm intensity. It would be crazy to be in a position of having to pay off infrastructure bonds long after a facility is no longer useable because we didn't think twice about climate change risks. Instead, by factoring the risks associated with climate change into infrastructure planning, safer locations or new designs for new facilities might be selected.

- As we think about the possibility of a lot more hot days (over 95 degrees Fahrenheit) every summer, what improvements might we make in public and elderly housing that would help people without air conditioning survive? It should be possible to design or retrofit public housing units and to add trees and plantings to keep these units cooler. It should also be possible to designate public cooling centers along with ways of helping the disabled get to these locations during a heat wave. Many lives could be saved. These are things worth considering regardless of whether anyone is sure that the increase in the number of hot summer days over the past decade was caused by climate change. People died in Chicago several years ago because of what is now called "the heat island effect."

When you get into improvisational discussions or brainstorming sessions with skeptics, avoid asking yes or no questions. Instead ask when, where, and how questions. How could we reduce certain risks while accomplishing other worthwhile goals? When we have the information in hand, and the public dialogue that follows can look at the full range of costs and benefits (and I don't just mean in dollar terms) what kinds of choices might be made? People with very different views about what climate change science allows us to know might still agree on useful steps to take to reduce the risks associated with climate change because these same activities would help them achieve other things they see as important.

Don't personalize these discussions. Focus on outcomes that would respect everyone's principles. Talk to people you disagree with in the same way you would like to have them talk to you.

Don't paint people into corners by saying something like, "Since science knows Fact A to be true, then you must agree that everyone ought to take Action 1." That will just provoke a counterattack along the lines that there must be someone (somewhere on the Web) who disagrees with Fact A. Moreover, everyone who agrees that Fact A is true will not agree that only Action 1 is the logical thing to do. Instead, say, "Forget for a moment whether Fact A is true or not. What are things that people who don't necessarily agree about Fact A would suggest are worth doing for a variety of reasons?"

Attentiveness, flexibility, playfulness, and an ability to take advantage of surprises are all valuable skills in dealing with climate change skeptics or negotiating with anyone who disagrees with you. As my colleague Michael Wheeler points out, negotiators who stick too closely to a script are unlikely to find their way into the trading zone or to win at win-win negotiation. Improvisation may be one of the most important tools for formulating agreements that are good for them and great for you.

DON'T LIKE SURPRISES? USE CONTINGENT AGREEMENTS

THE TOWN GOVERNMENT of "Pleasantview" and the private fuel-oil company "High-Energy, Inc." have a standing contract that they have renewed for several years in a row. The contract is again up for renewal, and the town manager is under pressure from a substantial portion of the citizenry to reduce heating costs and avoid tax increases. The town's fuel-oil consumption has remained relatively stable during the past five years, yet costs have shot up almost 60 percent. As a longtime client, Pleasantview feels it should get some protection from sudden price jumps.

The town manager hits on the idea of asking the company to provide a guaranteed annual price increase cap of 10 percent in exchange for agreed-upon delivery dates and amounts for the life of the contract. With a price cap in place, the town would not have to increase its fuel-oil budget by more than a certain amount each year. Although the town might have to pay a slightly higher per-gallon cost over the life of the contract in exchange for the consumption guarantee, this would be a reasonable tradeoff. High-Energy has never agreed to a price cap for a municipal customer, but it ultimately agrees to the manager's requests for fear of losing the business and facing negative publicity.

The price cap proposed by the town manager is a type of contingent agreement, in which a range of "If this happens, then we do this or that" promises are added to a negotiated contract to reduce risk in the face of real-life uncertainty about the future. Whenever negotiators strike a deal, both sides must make forecasts and assumptions. Will current conditions remain the same or change after the agreement is signed? Will the other side hold up its end of the bargain? By including contingent incentives or penalties in a contract, you can protect yourself from the risk that your negotiating partner will renege on a commitment as well as improve the prospects of compliance.

Some argue that contingencies unnecessarily complicate business contracts and other kinds of agreements. It's true that contingent agreements can add complexity to a negotiation; but with a little preparation, the benefits will far outweigh the costs.

When to Use Contingent Agreements

NEGOTIATORS CAN USE contingent agreements for several reasons, including making commitments more self-enforcing, managing technical disagreements, avoiding the need to reconvene if difficult circumstances arise, and reducing the chances of future litigation.

Make commitments self-enforcing. In negotiating agreements of all kinds, it's a good idea to seek protection against possible surprises—broad changes that may occur through no fault or effort on the part of either side, such as fluctuations in market demand, prices, laws, policies, or technological innovations. When all the different "futures" are spelled out clearly at the time the contract is signed, contingent agreements have a useful self-enforcing quality: they can increase the durability of contracts by eliminating the need to reconvene or renegotiate whenever surprises occur.

Contingencies often create incentives for compliance as well as penalties for noncompliance. Professional athletes negotiate with their team owners for contractual performance bonuses. When hiring a contractor to build an expensive addition onto your house, you might add a contingency that rewards the contractor with a prenegotiated bonus if his team beats a certain deadline. Cities often ask developers to post a bond equal to the amount it would take to complete all the public services associated with an approved plan. The city doesn't liquidate the bond until the developer has met all its obligations.

Insurance also can be viewed as a type of contingent agreement because it increases the security of contractual arrangements in an ever-changing world. A company invited to build a plant in an area highly susceptible to hurricane damage might want to ask the local government to purchase an insurance policy that would protect the company against a future disaster in return for its efforts to facilitate economic development.

Resolve technical disagreements. Negotiations often get hung up on technical considerations. Suppose that an oil company seeking a permit to build a new refinery promises to keep various environmental disruptions to a minimum. Not surprisingly, local residents worry that the refinery owners won't live up to their commitments and that regulatory agencies will be lax or inefficient in tracking possible violations. What if an accident does occur? Maybe the company would prefer to pay a small fine rather than hold its facility to the highest possible standards. Meanwhile, the oil company might dispute whether the community's informal observations and measurements were valid.

A contingent agreement could reduce the likelihood of such disagreements. If the company is confident that its plant will operate safely and cleanly, why not agree to address the residents' concerns? A "good neighbor" agreement could include detailed monitoring and shutdown provisions beyond those required by law. The oil company might even agree to train and fund local residents in monitoring techniques, thereby avoiding future battles between independent experts. Through contingent provisions, both sides can reduce the risk of technical disagreements that might eventually lead to conflict.

Plan to reconvene. When one side suspects that the other has failed to live up to contractual promises, it might want to reconvene to discuss the possible breach. Negotiators can avoid such potentially awkward encounters in advance by setting fixed dates to meet and review progress during the life of a contract. It's easier to agree to undertake a joint investigation and sort out what needs to be done at a prescheduled session than at a time when one side is claiming violation of contract terms.

In the construction world, such partnering agreements—in which the contractor and the client agree to meet periodically to maintain or improve their working relationship—are quite common. If no effort is made to enhance relationships before problems arise—especially once charges and countercharges have been leveled—it becomes all the more difficult to clarify misunderstandings and build greater trust.

Head off litigation. To reduce the likelihood of going to court at the first sign of difficulty, consider carefully spelling out informal dispute-handling clauses in your contracts. Typically, such contingencies stipulate that both sides must continue to meet their contractual obligations until a neutral party has investigated any potential violations. Without such measures, contractual charges and countercharges can take on a self-fulfilling quality.

If I think you're not living up to your end of our bargain, I might unilaterally disengage from the contract. Of course, if it turns out that I was mistaken, my contract breach would be reason enough for you to shed your obligations as well.

The advantages of contingent agreements might seem to qualify them as a normal step in any serious negotiation. All too often, however, this is not the case. But there are four steps

---

CONTINGENT AGREEMENTS:

- *Make commitments more self-enforcing*
- *Resolve technical disagreements*
- *Plan to reconvene*
- *Head off litigation*

you can take to overcome internal resistance to contingent agreements fairly easily.

Raise red flags. During negotiations don't be afraid to bring up concerns about things that might possibly go wrong in the future; point out that such predictable surprises can be handled with contingent agreements. Resist the charge that you're being pessimistic or increasing the odds of trouble simply by looking at what might go wrong. Rather, argue that you are being optimistic: you believe it's possible to make durable agreements that can traverse all kinds of bumps in the road.

Strive for self-enforcing agreements. By including incentives and disincentives, you'll make it more likely that everyone involved will live up to their commitments without the need for messy, expensive enforcement proceedings. Prearranged incentives and penalties for meeting or exceeding contract terms foster not only effective negotiation but also effective implementation.

Accept disagreement. Don't worry if you and your negotiating partner disagree on what the future may hold. Contingent agreements allow you to sidestep the need to agree on whose forecast is most accurate. Create one possible scenario that describes what the other side assumes will happen. Next, outline your own scenario of what you think is more likely to happen. Finally, spell out expectations and requirements appropriate to each scenario. Include both scenarios in the contract. In doing so, you'll create an agreement that all sides can live with. Added complexity is a small price to pay, as long as clear triggers and monitoring arrangements state exactly when and why one scenario or another kicks in.

Forecast benefits. To overcome organizational resistance to contingent agreements, you'll have to describe the benefits that balance the costs of complexity. The legal and financial experts who prefer less complexity are just trying to do their jobs. But if you can show them how multiple contingent scenarios can head off potential crises, you can head off their defense of simplicity for its own sake. Contingent agreements offer an easy way to win at win-win negotiation. You put the terms you prefer into the agreement—based on your forecast of what is most likely to happen—and the other side accepts them, along with their alternative forecast (which you don't think is correct) coupled with the conditions they prefer. Assuming your forecast is correct, you've won the value distribution battle without a fight.

WHAT'S SPECIAL ABOUT TECHNOLOGY-RELATED AND OTHER KINDS OF COMPLEX NEGOTIATIONS?

CONTINGENT AGREEMENTS CAN BE especially helpful in coping with the uncertainty surrounding technical issues such as finance and software, realms about which executives may know very little. Whether you're bargaining over the purchase of a new companywide computer network, coping with a possible infringement of patented technology, or seeking better customer service from a software supplier, uncertainty is a fact of managerial life.

How do negotiations about complex systems differ from those that are less technologically complex? You can anticipate that four specific problems will crop up more often in the technology arena:

1. **Complexity.** Negotiations over complex systems such as new technology require sophisticated knowledge of hardware or software that's beyond the expertise of most managers. If those trained in science and technology assume that others at the table speak their language, serious misunderstandings can result. Often technical advisers talk over the heads of non-tech people, and less technically sophisticated managers agree to things they don't fully understand.

2. **Uncertainty.** When highly complex systems are at stake, no one can be sure whether they will perform as promised, especially when configured for a particular business environment. Different estimates of how a technology will perform can lead to long, drawn-out negotiations.

3. **Egos.** People who design or advocate for a new technology often become additional players when they have a vested interest in the outcome of a negotiation. Technology advocates—and their egos—can complicate otherwise straightforward talks.

4. **Organizational change.** The various organizational changes that often come with the introduction of a new technology can provoke conflict between parties during implementation. Staffers may have trouble maintaining or repairing new technology, accessing its intellectual underpinnings, or acquiring replacement parts.

Negotiators embroiled in a high-tech deal must find purposeful ways of avoiding these pitfalls. I have identified three primary strategies that will help you sidestep them—avoiding communication errors and building trust, managing uncertainty using contingent agreements, and preparing for strategic realignment—which I will discuss below. But first, a vignette to illustrate them.

"Cremtech Corporation," which develops and manufactures leading-edge glass and ceramic products, was considered the industry leader in terms of innovation and profits for many years. Recently, however, Cremtech has faced growing competition, and its profits have slipped. The company's CEO has asked senior management to eliminate technologies that have not found significant markets or applications. Such technologies drain production capacity and create heavy handling, shipping, and customer support costs.

"Advanceramics," a Cremtech competitor, recently offered $2.5 million for Cremtech's "Hexiglass" line of extrudable glass products (products made by molding glass using a die). Hexiglass, which has only six customers who order twelve products, is manufactured and sold by twelve employees. If selling the line isn't feasible, Advanceramics is willing to license the production technology for two years.

Three senior managers at the facility where Hexiglass is produced have been asked to negotiate the product's future: the product line manager for specialty ceramics, the vice president of R&D, and the plant manager. Not surprisingly, they have different ideas about whether to accept the offer from Advanceramics. The R&D VP, who invented Hexiglass, is strongly opposed to selling the technology. He wants to mothball Hexiglass, store it on site, keep the team in place, and test new applications until demand skyrockets, as he is convinced it will.

The product line manager wants to accept the Advanceramics offer. The sale of Hexiglass, she believes, will bring in cash and increase short-term productivity. In addition, she hopes to impress the CEO with her ability to pull the trigger on a good deal.

The plant manager doesn't want to lay off veteran employees; he favors licensing Hexiglass technology for a short-term cash infusion and keeping the team together. If demand grows rapidly, as the product manager predicts, Cremtech will be ready to restart production immediately. Notably, the legal department is worried about the intellectual property risks associated with any licensing agreement.

Though this negotiation is among people working for the same company, it exhibits the four problems salient to technology deals—and, as it happens, the same problems that would arise in talks between Cremtech and Advanceramics. First, the varying extent to which the negotiators understand the technology is likely to color their views of the three options—sell, mothball, or license. Second, uncertainty surrounds long-term demand for the product, as well as the question of whether shutting down Hexiglass production would increase plant efficiency. If demand truly will skyrocket, then mothballing the technology makes sense. But if the R&D VP is wrong, Cremtech may never get another bid on the technology. Third, ego becomes a factor: the R&D VP may be blinded by "inventor's bias." Similarly, the product manager's major objective seems to be impressing her boss and the plant manager wants to retain veteran employees. Fourth, temporarily licensing the technology could lead to unanticipated organizational realignment as staff reassignments and the need to build a new relationship with Advanceramics create additional demands. If the competition ends up launching its own version of the product, further changes will be required.

Given these complications, how should the managers proceed with their negotiation? The following three strategies will help them navigate these difficulties—and they can guide your next technology or other complex negotiation as well.

Avoid Communication Errors and Build Trust

BECAUSE OF THEIR COMPLEXITY, technology-related deals are rife with miscommunication. Negotiators tend to make assumptions about a technology—how it will work, what its future demand will be—that color their messages and leave them more likely to hear what they want to hear and block out the rest.

Negotiators can avoid miscommunication about technology by agreeing on explicit procedural ground rules before getting down to substantive business. For example, the three Cremtech negotiators might agree that: (1) they will present their arguments without interruption, (2) one person will draft a discussion summary for review by the full group before speaking to others about what transpired, and (3) they will use specific criteria to assess alternatives. Procedural ground rules not only promote understanding but also improve the odds of reaching a creative agreement that responds to each party's key concerns.

To better understand one another, the Cremtech managers should find out all they can about the rationale behind the other side's proposal and the reasons they disagree about it. This is best done by asking lots of questions and listening carefully to the answers. In addition, the managers should use simple, jargon-free language to make their points and supplement their statements with visual aids whenever possible. Finally, rather than merely observing others' reactions, they should ask for elaboration on any points of disagreements.

Often, the advocate for a particular system (whether that person designed it or not) becomes blind to the weaknesses of that technology. The R&D VP's ego, for instance, could make it hard for him to listen without defensiveness if a message appears to threaten his identity or reputation. To neutralize a situation involving inventor's bias, bring in an impartial expert to provide an independent judgment of the technology's strengths and weaknesses. Similarly, the Cremtech negotiators might seek an independent financial analysis from a consultant who is less concerned than the product line manager with impressing the boss.

Whenever technical complexity threatens to impede communication, it's important to emphasize trust-building measures. Negotiations about complex topics such as technology often require multiple rounds of give-and-take, as parties check with their legal departments or superiors in response to unexpected proposals. Trust can break down quickly during these interactions—for example, if one party alters a previous offer. How can you build trust? Quite simply, by saying what you mean and meaning what you say. Don't sugarcoat bad news, and don't make commitments that you're not sure you can keep. Once trust is lost, it's incredibly difficult to rebuild.

Manage Complexity and Uncertainty

PRIOR TO A NEGOTIATION, it's in everyone's interest to learn all they can about the technology under discussion. This may require a substantial investment of time. Even if you're planning to bring a technical adviser to the meetings, you'll still need a rough sense of the technical or scientific principles involved, the options available, and the obstacles to effective implementation.

Negotiators also need to make time pressures and ambiguity work for them. The idea of mothballing the Hexiglass technology until the market catches up may well be a smart response to market uncertainty. By contrast, leasing the technology might bring in short-term revenue, although even the strongest contract won't eliminate the possibility that a competitor will use its access to formulate its own version of the technology. Both ideas respond to uncertainty, but with different downside risks.

In my research, I've discovered that those who can live with ambiguity a little longer are more likely to reap substantial benefits than are those who seek to quickly eliminate it. One novel way to accept uncertainty is by making contingent offers, as discussed above—promises that negotiators add to sidestep differences regarding what the future may hold. A contingent agreement might include a table that accounts for many future scenarios, including different prices, deadlines, and obligations for different versions of the same basic agreement. Contingencies add complexity and sometimes, as noted earlier, incur the wrath of a general counsel whose job it is to define and limit company liability. They also make it difficult to book the value of the deal (and allocate bonuses) when an agreement is signed. Nevertheless, when uncertainty is high, all parties will be best served by spelling out who gets what under a variety of scenarios. Whosever forecast turns out to be right gets what they expected. The others can turn to the schedule of alternatives and be clear about what they will get as well.

Anticipate the Difficulties of Strategic Realignment

ALMOST ANY AGREEMENT the Cremtech negotiators reach will require ongoing organizational realignment. New staff members probably will have to be trained, while longtime employees must be let go. Managers may need to reassign responsibilities, adjust reporting lines, and impose performance guidelines. The company may have to alter supply chains and invest in retraining. Such strategic moves will disrupt relationships and work patterns—and make a lot of people uneasy. And while most negotiators expect organizational change to be difficult, agreements about complex areas such as technology rarely take adequate account of the strategic realignment likely to be required.

When these negotiations imply changes in organizational structure, values, and procedures, you'll need to approach them with a clear understanding of the organizational (not just personal) stakes involved. Specifically, follow three "before, during, and after" steps. First, consult in advance with anyone likely to be affected by potential changes. Second, stay in touch with those individuals during the negotiation, and consider giving them a say in the final outcome. Third, make sure your promises about what you will and won't accomplish in the near future are realistic.

Merely insisting on or promising organizational change is unlikely to produce the desired results. When you're altering systems, strategy, or values, resistance is almost inevitable. Getting people to change what they think, what they do, and how they do it is usually a grueling exercise. In addition, someone must be responsible for managing technological change and guaranteeing the resources needed to get the job done.

THREE STEPS TO NAVIGATING YOUR WAY THROUGH
HIGH-TECH NEGOTIATIONS:

- *Avoid communication errors and build trust*
- *Manage complexity and uncertainty*
- *Anticipate the difficulties of strategic alignment*

Three Ways to Be More Effective at Technology Negotiation

SINCE NEGOTIATIONS ABOUT TECHNOLOGY are complex, they are particularly susceptible to miscommunication and misunderstanding. To increase the chances of winning at win-win negotiation when technology is the focus, there are a few prescriptions I can offer:

1. **Acknowledge strategic conflicts.** Organizations do well by assigning different people to care about different goals and objectives (e.g., cost reduction, innovation, customer service, quality). When these goals conflict, it is essential to create a forum for discussion in which everyone's goals and concerns are valued, so that options for mutual gain are more likely to emerge.

2. **Similarly, if you value working relationships, be careful about appealing to "what's best for the company."** Be especially cautious if doing so means asking someone to incur real loss or risk without acknowledgment, compensation, or realigned performance measures. Keep in mind that "what's best for the company" will be judged from each manager's particular perspective, no matter what initiative is being advanced.

3. **Don't waste time arguing about who has the better crystal ball.** Technology platforms and materials, market conditions, and innovation all create a difficult forecasting environment. Instead, develop proposals that include contingent agreements in the form of "If X, then Y." Different expectations or beliefs about the future can be handled efficiently in this way.

WRITE THEIR VICTORY SPEECH
Help the Other Side Sell Your Best Deal to Their Back Table

BUILD BOTH OFFENSIVE AND DEFENSIVE COALITIONS

NOTHING IS EVER AS SIMPLE as it seems, including most two-party negotiations. They're actually multiparty negotiations because, in addition to the people negotiating at the table, there are back tables involved. Every savvy negotiator knows he has to find a way to appeal to the other side's back table—to build a winning coalition with them. They are the ones who have to approve whatever the terms of the final deal might be.

Then there are situations in which there really are more than two parties (not counting back tables). Keeping track of the interests of multiple parties (including multiple back tables) and building a winning coalition can be difficult. Moreover, this often has to be accomplished while others are trying to form winning coalitions without you. Building a winning coalition or a partnership with your negotiating counterpart's back table or with others in a multiparty negotiation requires careful preparation. You need a way to get others to see that your proposal is so much better for them than no agreement and that they can't afford to turn you down.

You should focus both on offense—how to build a winning coalition (i.e., how to get the other side's back table or others around the table on your side)—and defense—how to organize a blocking coalition that can, if necessary, thwart your negotiating counterparts' efforts to build a winning coalition without you.

Two-party and multiparty negotiations share one important feature: finding the trading zone as quickly as possible, so you can move on to proposing deals or packages of trades that are a little better for others than their next best option while being a lot better for you than your walk-away.

If you're trying to move your counterparts' back tables into the trading zone, you will need to: closely attend to their needs and interests, put forward proposals that incorporate value-creating benefits for them, offer strong arguments on behalf of the package you are suggesting, and agree on problem-solving procedures that will cause your counterparts' back tables to push them to accept your proposal.

Preparing for Multiparty Negotiation

IT IS IMPORTANT to pay close attention to potential conflicts or differences between the interests of your counterparts at the table and their back tables. Similarly, if you see a blocking coalition forming, you need to be able to estimate what their back tables are likely to end up with, and top it. Assessing the other sides' walk-aways means putting yourself in their shoes: gathering the same kind of information you needed to make the same kind of estimates for yourself. When you've gotten a fix on someone else's best alternative to a negotiated agreement, you've identified the bare minimum you need to offer them to get them to say yes. You don't want to offer more than you have to. You don't need to provide everything they want; you need only to match what their realistic walk-away will leave them with. Of course, your negotiating counterparts may be willing to gamble. They might be willing to pursue a very small chance that if they turn down your perfectly reasonable offer, some unknown negotiating partner or opportunity will appear and offer them something even better. The time when they are thinking along these lines is when you need to get a message to their back table, letting them know that their negotiator is on the verge of turning down your very reasonable offer for a highly unlikely bet.

Internal circumstances on the other side might cause your counterparts to feel that it is in their best interest to take a chance on a highly unlikely but dramatic win. If their back tables knew what their negotiators had in mind, they might prefer that they take your offer. So you need to determine when your negotiating counterpart or a blocking coalition is operating on their own, without the full knowledge and support of their back tables, and how you might get a message to their back tables and build a winning coalition with them. Sometimes this can be done by offering your negotiating counterparts two starkly different packages, both acceptable to you, with the requirement that they check with their back tables. You could say that you want to know which of your two proposals should be the basis for ongoing negotiations. Indicate that you will check with your back table, and you want them to do the same.

For example, consider a merger being negotiated by the CEOs of two airlines, "FlyAway" and "Destinations." Neither CEO is dissatisfied with the status quo, but their boards

of directors have been pushing them to "do something to reduce the challenges posed by the competition." If FlyAway and
Destinations decide to merge, one CEO might lose his job,
and more than one segment of one or both companies might
be eliminated. As a result, each CEO has to compare the status quo (which is increasingly less profitable) with a variety of
two-way mergers—some of which will create strong push-back
internally and might involve one of them losing his job. The
board of directors of both FlyAway and Destinations might be
happy with a possible merger, but one of the two CEOs might
not be. The CEO who manages to build a coalition with the
other side's back table is most likely to win this negotiation. A
smart negotiator in this situation needs to be very sure where
he stands with his own back table. Then, he needs to put forward multiple deals that the CEO on the other side will have
no choice but to show to his or her back table. Your goal as the
CEO negotiator in this situation is first to build a coalition with
your own back table and then to build a winning coalition with
your counterpart's back table by offering a deal that is good for
them and great for you.

Anticipating Coalitional Behavior

A SECOND EXAMPLE of what it takes to build a winning coalition
involves "Community Arts, Inc.," a regional arts council. Mu-
seums, after-school groups, community colleges, and others in
more than thirty communities banded together in an effort to
expand philanthropic and corporate support for the arts. The
council has a new chairperson, and more than half the members
of the council have become united in opposition to the branding and fundraising strategy she recently announced. On the
advice of a private strategic planning company, she proposed a

series of high-profit but expensive events built around local celebrities. Her opponents not only felt that a small number of high-cost events was too risky, but also objected to a celebrity-driven strategy. They knew their clout would be enhanced if they could speak with one voice. In the early days of her tenure, the chair spent most of her time with staff developing her fundraising ideas and not enough time sounding out council members and winning their support for the reforms she had in mind.

The chair's misstep highlights the first rule of coalition building: think carefully about how to invest your time identifying and winning over possible coalition partners. As you talk with each potential coalition member, you may be asked to make tentative commitments before you know all the possible partners and what they might want. Before making commitments, ask yourself two key questions: (1) How will we divide up whatever value we are able to create? (In this case, if her fundraising strategy is successful, how will money be allocated among the competing priorities of the council members?) (2) Should I commit to a pretty good split with an initial set of coalition partners before hearing what others have to offer? I'm afraid the chair was not thinking at all about two important issues: what it would take to build a winning coalition, and, if her strategy were successful, what she would promise to potential coalition partners.

At the early stages of coalition building, your goal should be to collect relatively firm commitments from potential coalition partners while retaining sufficient flexibility to switch allegiances if necessary. This can be delicate, but the results are well worth the effort.

The perils of failing to build coalitions played out on a global scale more than a decade ago. Facing an important round of World Trade Organization negotiations in Cancún, Mexico, the U.S. government approached the European Union and a handful of its other usual partners from the developed world. Together, this informal coalition hammered out a preliminary agreement among themselves focused on how agricultural subsidies should be handled by wealthy nations. Usually, the WTO is against any system of subsidies that impedes free trade. Noticeably absent from these preconference talks were members of the G22, the coalition of rapidly growing developing nations like India, Brazil, and China.

Once the WTO talks were officially under way, it quickly became apparent that the developed nations had made a crucial miscalculation by leaving the developing world out of their preconference coalition. The G22 wanted a commitment from the developed nations that they would reduce the subsidies they provide to their own farmers. (These subsidies make it harder for developing countries that want to export their agricultural products to the United States and Europe.) The wealthy nations were not prepared to make a deal, and the developing world was insulted by the developed world's failure to take its concerns seriously. Talks broke down, and all sides walked away empty-handed. The lesson for all multiparty negotiators: choose your coalition partners wisely!

Face-to-face conversation among potential allies, or coalition building, requires close attention to the dynamics of group interaction.

Managing Group Interactions

WHEN MULTIPLE PARTIES GATHER to discuss a packed agenda, the process can descend into chaos or stalemate, making it difficult to find the trading zone or build a winning coalition. It's usually too much to expect that one of the parties will be able to manage the conversation in an even-handed way. If one party, however well intentioned, tries to assume the role of chair, others may view that as a power grab. And in multiparty negotiation, process opportunism—the possibility that a manager or faction will wrest control of the agenda—is a constant worry.

Right from the start of multiparty talks, the parties may want to enlist a trained neutral—a professional facilitator or mediator. Some people think you bring in a mediator only after a dispute has erupted. But the fact is, a neutral party can guide participants into the trading zone much more effectively than they can find it on their own. (More on this in chapter 5.) Neutrals can be particularly helpful in the information-gathering stage. Through a process of joint fact-finding (as discussed in chapter 1), a mediator can help parties generate data and forecasts that everyone can use to build proposals or packages.

As the number of parties in a negotiation increases, group management becomes a bigger challenge. One factor is the phenomenon known as "groupthink," a term coined by psychologist Irving Janis. When people work together, sometimes their wish for unanimity overrides their commitment to weighing alternatives carefully. In their desire to please the group, participants are sometimes persuaded to accept solutions that are not in their own best interest. For this reason, negotiators in multiparty situations need to remain in close contact with their back tables. Otherwise, the pressure at the table to reach agreement may cause them to lose touch with the interests they are supposed to be representing.

When multiple parties are considering numerous issues at the same time, it often makes sense to break into smaller working groups. For example, when multiple companies or units are considering a possible merger, they might create separate working groups, populated by experts from all sides, to consider a range of technical issues. These subgroups contribute their findings to the larger conversation. That is, they don't have decision-making responsibility. Also, they must communicate their input in a way that is understandable to others who are not as well versed in specific technical issues as they are. But the packages that emerge, once the separate pieces have been put together, are more likely to be credible to all sides if they are prepared through appropriately structured working groups.

IN MULTIPARTY NEGOTIATIONS:

- *Prepare*
- *Anticipate coalitional behavior*
- *Manage group interactions*

Prospering in a Multiparty Trading Zone

WITH THOROUGH PREPARATION, the help of a trained mediator, and useful reports from subgroups, participants in a multiparty negotiation should be able to find their way to the trading zone. Once they have arrived, the next step, of course, is to work together to ensure that everyone's interests are met, even as each side tries to win.

To prosper in a multiparty trading zone, you need to pursue a coalitional strategy, building alliances to increase your leverage. It is important to do this in a way that doesn't undermine relationships with those who may have started out as your antagonists in a blocking coalition, only to emerge as potential members of your winning alliance. When others approach you about joining their coalition, be sure to respond with caution and tact, especially when you are approached by emissaries from the back tables of other negotiators.

When a large group has succeeded in generating possible proposals or package deals, how should they decide which one prevails? Clarify the way the group intends to make a final decision. In a negotiation with many parties (not just two parties and their back tables), a commitment to unanimity as a decision rule is probably a mistake. It certainly invites blackmail by those who care more about a pet issue or a personal advantage than the overall success of the negotiation. Majority voting is also undesirable (as was explained in chapter 2) since a significant number of parties can be boxed out entirely, leading to unstable agreements because disgruntled minorities may look for opportunities to sabotage implementation of whatever agreement emerged. Most of the time, agreement by an overwhelming majority—consensus agreement—is the best decision rule. Under such a rule, parties should strive to seek unanimity but settle for near-unanimous agreement after every effort has been made to meet everyone's interests. This is how coalitions win in multiparty negotiation.

Finally, keep in mind that the structure of the negotiating forum itself—that is, the ground rules that constrain the way a multiparty negotiation unfolds (even a two-party negotiation with back tables)—will be a constant topic of conversation. Negotiators need to be able to quickly size up and react to possible changes in coalitional dynamics. By paying close attention to the shifting walk-aways of all parties, as new coalitions emerge backing entirely new deals, multiparty negotiators can pursue their interests and win at win-win negotiation. This requires a commitment to building effective coalitions, often with the back tables of negotiating counterparts.

How these ideas play out can be seen in the daunting task of securing licenses and permits through negotiations with regulators. The odds of success are improved if you can force yourself to think the way they do. That is, you need to imagine what the victory speech might be that your counterpart can give to their back table once their negotiation with you is concluded.

NEGOTIATING WITH REGULATORS

WHEN PREPARING TO LAUNCH new products, plans, and innovations, an organization often must apply for licenses, permits, and other types of regulatory approvals from government agencies. Consider a few such instances:

- A pharmaceutical company is seeking a variety of approvals from federal regulators to bring a new drug to market. In its extensive interactions with regulators, the drug company must establish not only the costs and benefits of the new drug but also how such assessments should be made.
- To construct a mixed-use project, a real estate developer must apply for a number of municipal and state permits. In addition to putting forth a proposal that's consistent with published rules and regulations, the developer must cope with the larger community's concerns about congestion and pollution.

- A telecommunications company is about to negotiate with federal regulators over changes in the annual rates it will charge its customers. Given mounting customer dissatisfaction over service quality, even the company's most compelling economic analysis may not be sufficient to win regulatory approval.

Thankfully, even the most elaborate application processes allow individual regulators a measure of discretion, a fact that gives you multiple opportunities to negotiate with them—and, indeed, even requires that you do so. The four rules that follow will help you navigate a wide range of governmental settings, both in the United States and in other countries, and improve your odds of gaining approval. Indeed, the negotiation strategy that works with regulators—especially forcing yourself to think the way they do—can be helpful in many other contexts as well.

Think Like the People You Want to Influence

AS IN ANY NEGOTIATION CONTEXT, it helps to put yourself in the other side's shoes. When negotiating with a regulator, think like one. This will help you build a coalition with their back table. (Yes, even regulators have back tables!) Like any professional group, regulators have a mindset or beliefs that govern how they think about their work. Dealing with regulators—or any group for that matter—requires that you understand what's in their head. Here are four beliefs that most regulators share.

First, regulators assume they can do a good job only if they follow the letter of the law and treat everyone who has a similar request in exactly the same manner. If you are seeking state approval for a new building technology that has already been turned down (when a competitor sought approval), don't expect the agency to accept your application. You'll need to propose something sufficiently different so that the previous decision doesn't apply.

Second, regulators assume that they will have to account for the decisions they make, as well as for the reasons they made them. As a result, they are likely to treat every decision as if it sets a precedent. They will also be sure to create a paper trail that can be used to justify their actions.

Third, regulators assume that most applicants will try to cut corners to save time and money. This forces them to be on the lookout for applicants who skimp on supporting information or who fail to adequately answer required questions. It would be a mistake to try to minimize the burden on regulators by limiting the information you submit.

Fourth, regulators tend to be much less concerned about the net benefits associated with a specific proposal or project than with the extent to which you're following rules, procedures, and standards. From a regulator's standpoint, even small risks to the public loom larger than potential gains for proponents or the broader community.

To illustrate these beliefs, suppose that "GreenTech Chemical Company" asks state environmental regulators for permission to install a cleaner, "greener" waste treatment technology. GreenTech argues that if all goes well, the new equipment will substantially exceed the minimum environmental standards required by law and at lower costs than prevailing technologies. Regulators are likely to balk at this proposal, noting that the new technologies are not fully covered by published standards.

If the technologies fail to perform, the regulators will be singled out for blame.

In response, GreenTech might request contingent approval for a trial run of the new technology, with environmental organizations helping to evaluate the test results. Benchmarks would be set to assess whether results exceed current regulations and meet minimum safety requirements. When regulators learn that activist groups are involved in the proposal and that the trial run will not set a precedent, they may be willing to go along with the plan.

Assume That Regulators Have More Discretion Than They Admit

MOST REGULATORS WILL INSIST they have no freedom to interpret prevailing guidelines. Even if they could use their discretion to solve a problem in a novel way, they're unlikely to do so for fear of being viewed as making subjective or personal judgments. This is problematic because their professional identities hinge on the presumption of objectivity. Never act as if a regulator has the option of deciding which provisions to enforce and which to ignore.

Yet regulators actually do have a certain amount of discretion when it comes to interpreting guidelines, and they know that this discretion constitutes a source of power. Here are just a few of the types of judgment calls that regulators can make when processing your application:

- They can move quickly on an application or let it sit at the bottom of the stack.
- They can have a very experienced staff member handle your application or have a newcomer take care of it.

- They can make themselves available to you early in the process and alert you to mistakes, or they can meet only after you've submitted the application and reject it for containing incomplete data.
- They can share "model" applications that have won approval in the past or refrain from sharing such information.
- They can consider new independent scientific or technical studies on their merits or reject data from such studies on the grounds that their agency has not yet reviewed them.

Base Your Request on Past Approvals and Experiences

WHEN PROPOSING A NOVEL PRODUCT, service, or pricing strategy, look for elements of your proposal that have been approved in the past. Some aspects of what you're proposing may have already passed through the regulatory gauntlet in another context. Consultants with national or international experience may be able to provide this information. Regulators will take note if some other agency (perhaps in another country) has already approved what you're proposing.

When hiring technical consultants or experts, seek out those who have worked with that particular regulatory body before. This strategy will greatly increase the comfort level of the regulators involved.

Initiate Conversations Early in the Process

IT'S BETTER TO APPROACH REGULATORS before you've dotted every *i* and crossed every *t* in your application. Seeking help with an incomplete application gives you the time and space to respond to concerns that may not be clear in the published regulations. Spend time talking with lower-level professional staff at the agency about what you, as an applicant, can do to ensure adherence to the rules. (If you discuss such matters with higher-level staff, they may well respond by turning every information request into an official statement of agency policy.) Make clear that you're not asking for any sort of commitment, only a chance to brainstorm. Regulatory staff will tell you that it's not their job to solve your problems and that they can't offer opinions until you've submitted your final application. But during informal, off-the record conversations, they can help focus your attention on possible problems through the issues they raise.

Submitting multiple proposals early in the process is the best way to smoke out regulatory concerns. Instead of asking for a reaction to a specific technology or a radically new design, put forth several rough sketches and ask what's necessary to win approval of such designs. Staff comments on the strengths and weaknesses of each alternative will provide important clues as to what is likely to win approval. When you've finally submitted your application, don't attribute any changes that you may have incorporated to the regulatory staff that helped you.

Once you understand the regulatory agency's primary concerns about your proposal, it's often useful to proceed with some form of joint fact-finding. As described in chapter 1, this is a collaborative process in which negotiators with different agendas gather, analyze, and interpret information with the goal of reaching consensus on what is known and not known (even if they disagree on what ought to be done). Regulatory agencies can participate in joint fact-finding as long as it is not keyed to a specific pending proposal.

Suppose that a national agency is concerned about the health effects of a new pharmaceutical product. In such cases, it's usually a good idea to recruit stakeholder representatives and agency staff to oversee data collection to address those concerns in exploratory studies. A joint fact-finding process might delay your final application, and it will certainly impose additional costs, but it will almost always be worth the wait. Forecasts or analyses developed by both proponents and opponents are more likely to be taken seriously by regulators than those prepared solely by advocates of a given product.

Most government regulators want to be respected for their expertise, but they don't want to be asked to solve your problems for you. They want to be acknowledged as important players in decisions that fall under their auspices, but they don't want to be perceived as exercising subjective judgments. They don't want to engage in negotiations (which would imply that they have discretion), but they are almost always willing to talk with applicants before proposals are finalized. To summarize, the key to negotiating with regulators may be to avoid describing your discussions as negotiations!

How Not to Deal with Regulators

A MAJOR GROCERY CHAIN, "Cornucopia," wants to build a new superstore on a 10-acre parcel in a suburban town that lacks any sort of food store. Using the design of one of its most financially successful stores as a template, and without consulting local planning or public safety departments, the company files a completed application with the town seeking a special permit and site-plan approval to build a 65,000-square-foot supermarket with almost 300 parking spaces, a pharmacy, and a bank.

In the application, Cornucopia's consultants have tried to anticipate and answer every question that might be raised in a formal regulatory review. The company also hired a local attorney to meet informally with elected officials to explain why it would be in their interest to support the permit request. In addition, Cornucopia hired a PR firm to place a story in the local newspaper reporting the results of a survey indicating that a substantial percentage of residents favor the new market. When Cornucopia realizes that residents are worried about how traffic patterns might be affected, it commissions a study showing that any problems could be minimized with signs, lights, and curb cuts.

To the surprise of Cornucopia's management, local regulators rejected their permit application. Where did the company go wrong? First, the company should have met with town planning and public-safety professionals prior to submitting its formal proposal. Second, it should have modified its basic store design once it heard from residents and officials about their traffic concerns. Third, it should have organized a series

---

WHEN NEGOTIATING WITH REGULATORS,
IMPROVE YOUR ODDS OF APPROVAL BY:

- *Thinking like a regulator*
- *Assuming that regulators have more discretion than they admit*
- *Basing your request on past approvals and experiences*
- *Initiating conversations early in the process*

of community meetings to allow residents to ask questions and receive information about the project directly rather than from the newspaper and other second-hand sources. Fourth, it should have initiated joint fact-finding, perhaps by offering to fund a traffic-impact study by the town.

Negotiating with regulators means helping them sell your proposal to their back table and building a winning coalition. GreenTech and Cornucopia made no such efforts. They probably did not even imagine that regulatory staff had back tables to whom they were accountable. If you think like a regulator, you can help them make your case to their back table.

MEDIATION AS PROBLEM SOLVING

AS NOTED EARLIER, parties in complex negotiations can move into the trading zone with the help of mediators in ways they may not be able to on their own. And, once in the zone, the parties can get help from a mediator as they try to create value and, ultimately, as each attempts to win at win–win negotiation (without harming their long-term relationship).

The Organization for Economic Cooperation and Development (OECD) is supposed to hold multinational corporations to high standards of corporate social responsibility. The OECD member states are thirty-four of the major economies of the world. More than a decade ago, they adopted guidelines regarding human rights, environmental protection, the rights of workers, and child protection that all their member countries agreed to respect. Recently, the OECD directors undertook a ten-year review of those guidelines. During the previous decade, member countries appointed agencies called National Contact Points

(NCPs) to investigate claims that multinational corporations headquartered in their country, or their subsidiaries, wherever they might be located, have violated the guidelines. The NCPs have investigated as best they can (often with very limited staffs and budgets). The assumption is that being called out by their national government will push a multinational to correct whatever guideline infractions they or their subsidiaries may have committed. On some occasions, NCPs have not found sufficient evidence that the guidelines have been violated. In others, though, corporations have clearly violated the guidelines.

At a meeting of all the NCPs and some of their constituent organizations (including their Trade Union Advisory Group, their Business and Industry Advisory Group, and OECD Watch), the NCPs reaffirmed that their goal is to rectify inappropriate practices, not just determine whether guidelines have been violated. More generally, the NCPs were urged to step back from their adjudicatory (or investigatory) efforts and emphasize their problem-solving capabilities. In particular, they were urged to take their mediation mandate seriously. If you were a multinational corporation charged with violating global social responsibility standards, you would probably prefer a chance to correct the situation rather than wait for an embarrassing reprimand from the national government in your home country. For that to happen, though, quite a few parties need to come to the negotiating table.

Mediation can provide valuable assistance in such situations. I am especially supportive of a problem-solving approach to mediation. In too many situations, mediation is viewed as the last step in adjudication—that is, when impasse has been reached—rather than as the first step in a collaborative effort to work out a creative resolution of conflicting claims. When a complaint is filed, an NCP must determine whether the charges should be taken seriously. It sometimes does this by asking its national embassy to make inquiries about the local reputation of the company against whom the complaint has been filed. Then, it might follow up with a call to the company and ask for its version of the story. In short, the NCP tries to determine whether the company has, in fact, violated the OECD corporate social responsibility guidelines. They proceed in this way because their primary goal is to determine the legitimacy of the claim that has been brought. In the past two years, the NCPs have begun experimenting with mediation to resolve specific complaints.

Now that some NCPs see their goal as correcting inappropriate practices or implementing appropriate remedies, they have selected qualified mediators—located in the places where infractions supposedly have occurred—to meet informally with the relevant parties to see what solution can be worked out. The more informal the interaction, the less likely the parties have been to overstate their claims or react defensively. A problem-solving approach to mediation seeks to bring the parties into the trading zone and shift from assessing blame to creating value. From the standpoint of a company charged with violating the OECD guidelines, winning in such a situation might include garnering positive publicity (for cooperating) and improved relations with a national government whose support is crucial to expanding business operations.

If you were a company accused of violating OECD guidelines, wouldn't you prefer to meet privately with a neutral party (who would keep what you said confidential) rather than have to defend yourself in a public way as an official investigation gets under way? From the standpoint of preserving your corporate image, mediation is certainly preferable. If you were a trade union or an environmental NGO concerned about the actions of a multinational company in your area, wouldn't you prefer to have a professional mediator bring everyone together to respond to your concerns rather than wait a year or longer while an invisible agency—often in another part of the world—determines whether the OECD guidelines have been violated and then writes a report? Adjudication in the absence of enforcement (and that is the situation globally) cannot guarantee change. Mediation leading to voluntary agreements can guarantee compliance with whatever has been worked out—definitely an all-gain outcome.

Mediation (behind closed doors and with a promise of confidentiality) can be the best way of getting one side to accept a pretty good outcome while the other side gets a great outcome. Usually, in the current OECD context, a multinational that has violated OECD's corporate social responsibility guidelines is not going to admit publicly to doing so. However, if the product of a mediation effort involves a commitment to take a set of corrective actions without admitting that rules have been broken, those who want compensation or want the multinational's practices to change can get what they want (a very good outcome), while the multinational gets an acceptable outcome.

Mediation as problem-solving requires three things: (1) a willingness on the part of all the relevant stakeholders to work together to resolve a problem or deal with a situation, (2) the availability of a neutral with sufficient knowledge and skill to manage difficult conversations, and (3) an agreement on procedural ground rules (e.g., confidentiality, timetable, agenda, good faith effort, etc.).

I have been tracking some of the instances in which multinational corporations have been charged with violating OECD guidelines. In one case, the subsidiary of a European clothing company based in India was charged with refusing to let its workers unionize. While the case was pending in court in India, a complaint was filed in the national capital in Europe. The NCP decided that mediation rather than just an investigation of wrongdoing was called for. After the NCP met with the workers, the management of the Indian company, the leadership of the multinational in Europe, and other interested labor organizations, a resolution was worked out.

OECD's decision to use problem-solving mediation ought to ring some bells with smaller companies everywhere. If charges have been made that your company is out of compliance with health and safety regulations, rather than wait for an official investigation or a court case to unfold, you can initiate mediation. An appropriately qualified neutral can meet with all sides, help shape an agenda, bring the parties together, and work out a voluntary remedy. That's got to be a win for all sides. Anyone interested in winning at win-win negotiation should consider adding a mediator to the mix. You may be able to claim more and win at win-win negotiation if the terms of an agreement are worked out with the help of a mediator in a confidential context.

TO SOLVE PROBLEMS USING MEDIATION:

- *All parties have to be willing to work together*
- *A competent neutral professional should guide the process*
- *The parties must agree on procedural ground rules (e.g., confidentiality, good faith effort, etc.)*

PROTECT YOURSELF

Insulate Agreements against Predictable Surprises

NO MATTER HOW MUCH strategizing you do, almost every ne-gotiation will include some unexpected twists and turns. In the middle of a negotiation, for example, your counterpart may be replaced. Outside events, like a drop in the stock market or the emergence of a new competitor, may require recalibration of your negotiation strategy. Internal changes on your own side may require a shift in priorities. Although you can't plan for ev-ery possibility, you ought to proceed in a way that insulates you against an array of possible surprises—the kinds of things you are aware might happen—without knowing precisely which one will occur. You should negotiate in a way that gives you as much protection as possible.

BRINGING TALKS BACK ON TRACK WITH FACILITATION

AS MENTIONED IN THE PREVIOUS CHAPTER, one underappreciated and underutilized way to way to win at win-win negotiation is to bring in an outside mediator or facilitator (there are differ-ences between the two, as you will see below) who can help you and other parties create as much value as possible, maintain relationships, and help you respond to unexpected events. Let's look more closely at how a professional neutral actually works using a story from my experience. Bill and Dan shared a lucrative real estate business. After many years of constant bickering, they decided to call it quits. They were, however, not sure how to divide their joint holdings, each challenging the other's valuation of properties they really wanted. Bill and Dan finally agreed to get help from a mediator. (I must admit that I was the mediator.) After talking with them separately, I offered a low-cost solution that didn't involve paying for outside appraisals or fighting about the value of each property in their portfolio. I suggested that they flip a coin. The winner would get to choose any property he wanted from the list. The loser had the next choice, and they would keep going until all the properties were assigned. They followed this advice, and each was convinced he came out ahead. Neither had any basis to refute the other's claims. The mediation process took less than a day and helped the partners divide hundreds of millions of dollars worth of holdings. They loved telling the story about how they settled their dispute because it portrayed each of them as a risk-taker, since only the coin toss winner got to go first. With just that simple suggestion (based on my understanding of what made them tick), I offered them an inexpensive way to resolve their differences.

Managers often face similar situations—tempers flare, talks stall, anarchy threatens—especially when chairing tense meetings and complicated negotiations. As with the case of Bill and Dan, enlisting the help of a process expert, in this case a professional facilitator, might save the day.

Consider the dilemma faced by "Joe," the vice president of semiconductor technology at one of the largest computer companies in the world. His situation is similar to Brad's in the Best Care case described in chapter 2 (although Brad was focused on internal group conflict while Joe is dealing with external negotiations). One of Joe's many responsibilities includes chairing an alliance of representatives from six other large companies. Although the firms are heavily invested in competing with one another most of the time, the group works together to develop and acquire certain production technologies.

Unfortunately, Joe is the head of the alliance in name only; the other members second-guess every move he makes. What's more, months of difficult internal and external negotiations have caused the group to split into two warring factions. One wants to move quickly to purchase a recently patented software package from a small firm in Europe. The other is reluctant to make the buy, arguing that the software soon will be outmoded. Joe's own corporate interests have forced him to side with the first group, thereby undermining his ability to run the alliance evenhandedly.

After listening to Joe complain about the situation for many weeks, his assistant advises that he enlist the help of an outside professional facilitator. Facilitation is the process of guiding multiparty, multi-issue negotiations both within and outside an organization, often with the goal of heading off conflict or resolving a specific dispute.

Do You Need a Mediator or a Facilitator?

BUSINESSPEOPLE OFTEN USE the terms "facilitation" and "mediation" interchangeably, yet important distinctions exist between the two. It is smart to enlist the help of a mediator when your negotiation has already reached a standoff or when communication is entirely blocked, as was the case with Bill and Dan, or in the OECD case in the previous chapter. Professional mediators are generally expected to be strictly neutral and to bring a substantive knowledge of the issue under discussion to the table. Mediators also focus on getting the right people to the table and implementing the final deal.

By contrast, facilitation tends to be used at the beginning of a problem-solving negotiation, before a conflict has crystalized. In addition, the work of facilitation tends to be confined to what happens at the table when the parties are face-to-face. Facilitation can be viewed as a bundle of meeting management skills that anyone can employ, such as coordinating the flow of conversation, ensuring that participants observe time limits, cooling tempers when talks get overheated, and periodically summarizing the essence of emerging agreements.

When dealing with various conflicts that arise in negotiation, too many managers and organizations overlook the benefits of incorporating facilitation into their standard routines. As a result, they waste time and money—and risk escalating conflicts that could be resolved in their early stages.

Why Do Managers Resist Facilitation?

JOE IS RELUCTANT to hire a professional facilitator for at least three reasons—reasons that hold back many managers from seeking the assistance they need.

Fear of appearing incompetent. In Joe's company, senior managers are expected to be able to handle difficult conversations and negotiations on their own. Of course running a meeting may mean nothing more to some people than imposing an agenda and raising each item in turn. If your group is made up entirely of your direct reports, this approach might work. But when you are simply a titular chair, like Joe, with no authority over other group members, negotiation management requires joint problem-solving skills. These include knowing when and how to divide or combine issues to create value, when to encourage preparatory work away from the table, and when and how to insist that naysayers offer alternative proposals that everyone can accept. Unfortunately, no one ever taught Joe these skills. Clever though he may be, orchestrating a consensus-building effort that meets everyone's most important interests is not an intuitively obvious task for him.

Fear of looking weak. At some point during his professional career, Joe surmised that allowing (or, worse still, asking) someone to help run "his" negotiation session would be viewed as a sign of weakness. As a result, he worries that other alliance members will think they can walk all over him if he "abdicates control" to a professional facilitator. His self-image as a manager rests in large part on his ability to face down others whenever disagreements arise. In the past, his company has rewarded this warrior behavior. Better to lose with style, Joe thinks, than to cave in and be saddled with a reputation for weakness.

Fear of losing control. Joe is confused about how much authority a facilitator would have over alliance negotiations. His greatest fear is that once he hands over the gavel to an outsider, he will no longer influence the outcome of the group's debates.

In Joe's view, the best way to advance his and his company's interests is to exercise authority over other alliance members. In the past, his position as a chair has given him disproportionate influence over the agenda, the air time each participant receives, the spin put on group decisions, and even the substance of these decisions. While this has ceased to be the case, as other members have pushed back harder and harder, Joe's instinct is to fight even more fiercely to regain control.

When Facilitation Goes Wrong

FACILITATION WORKS ONLY when the facilitator is matched properly to the group and to the situation. The following signs of trouble may suggest that you need a different facilitator or that facilitation may not work for your group.

1. **Poor chemistry.** Your facilitator's personal style may be too forceful or not forceful enough for the group
2. **Lack of knowledge or experience.** Your facilitator may have great process management skills yet lack the organizational or institutional background needed to comprehend the issues facing the group.
3. **Lack of control.** If your group leader won't let the facilitator do her job, it's a mistake to go forward. Similarly, if your group members have different expectations of the facilitator's responsibilities, she won't succeed.
4. **Internal friction.** Underlying group divisions may make it impossible for any facilitator to proceed effectively. In these situations, members may try to blame the facilitator for their own failures.

5. **External pressures.** When a group is facing unreasonable deadlines, facilitation will probably fail. The group
   must be committed to taking at least the minimum
   amount of time required to work out differences.

Bringing a Professional Facilitator on Board

ON THE BRINK OF LOSING both the debate about the European
software acquisition and, in all likelihood, his leadership position in the alliance, Joe decides to take his assistant's advice. He
contacts a small facilitation firm recommended by the management school where he received his MBA. After meeting with
the head of the firm, Joe hires Claire, the firm's senior staff
member and an experienced facilitator. He then places informal
calls to each member of the alliance. To his surprise, no one
objects to Claire's attending the group's next meeting.

As the meeting begins, Claire spends a few minutes outlining her responsibilities. She explains that her role is simply to
help move the conversation along; she will not dictate the substance of group decisions. Tired of Joe's overbearing approach,
the members grant Claire speedy approval of the key elements
of a contract clarifying her duties. Her previous work history
in the software industry gives the members confidence that she
won't slow down their conversation.

Let's look more closely at the tasks Claire took on—and
why the alliance members, including Joe, end up having a very
positive experience with facilitation.

Working with the group to structure an agenda. Once
her contract was in place, Claire met individually with each

alliance member to find out as much as possible about his or her interests, priorities, and concerns. She promised to keep their disclosures confidential; that is, she indicated that she would not attribute any specific comments or suggestions to any particular member. Having had these conversations, Claire was prepared to shape an agenda with which everyone felt comfortable.

Setting and enforcing consensus-building ground rules. At her first working meeting with the group, Claire presented a short list of ground rules that the members quickly endorsed. Most reflected practices already in place—such as "Wait to be recognized before you start talking"—but some were new. For example, Claire promised to ensure that everyone would have a chance to discuss each agenda item at each meeting. She also promised to prepare draft summaries of all discussions and decisions, and to distribute them within twenty-four hours after each meeting. Each member was guaranteed a chance to make corrections to the summaries before they became final. Codifying these ground rules enabled Claire to move forward with the group's full support.

Capturing in writing a fair and accurate summary of a negotiated outcome. Whenever the group reached major decisions, Claire had the responsibility of producing a single written proposal incorporating everyone's suggestion for a package that would satisfy them all. When it came time to make a decision about the software purchase from the European company, Claire helped the group understand why the split in its ranks had occurred. Specifically, she noted that the two factions were so focused on their need to win that they misunderstood the source of their disagreement. With Claire's help, they negotiated a hard deadline for either producing their own shared version of the software or buying the European company's version.

Overcoming Resistance

JOE'S WORST FEARS never materialized. Claire didn't attempt to take over the meetings and didn't try to impose her views on the group. He retained his title as chair, and he was free to speak his mind and present his company's views in a straight-forward fashion. He also continued to handle all interactions with top brass at each member company, since Claire's role was limited to interactions with the alliance representatives at the meetings.

All alliance members contributed equally to Claire's fee, which was disbursed by Joe's company. From time to time, the group amended Claire's contract to reflect additional responsibilities they wanted her to assume. At one point, for instance, they asked her to coach them on how to improve their facilitation skills so that they could more effectively manage impromptu negotiations within their own companies.

PROFESSIONAL FACILITATORS HELP:

- *Structure agendas*
- *Set ground rules*
- *Keep the discussion focused and productive*
- *Record and summarize the discussion and outcomes*

Over time, the alliance became much more productive, allowing the group to reduce scheduled meetings from monthly to every other month and to rely on Claire to touch base with all members between talks. Indeed, the other alliance members made a point of congratulating Joe on having had the insight to hire Claire, and they became enthusiastic advocates of professional facilitation within their own companies.

DISPUTE PREVENTION: IT'S A GOOD IDEA, RIGHT?

I SAT ON A PANEL at the annual meeting of the International Institute for Conflict Prevention and Resolution in New York City. CPR has worked for more than thirty years to convince law firms and in-house corporate counsel to take dispute resolution seriously. One of CPR's great contributions is that they came up with the idea of adding a dispute resolution clause to all kinds of contracts so that parties don't resort to litigation at the first sign of disagreement. In a sense, a dispute resolution clause is a means of anticipating predictable surprises, that is, disputes that might arise during the course of implementing an agreement or a contract. The parties may not know exactly what disagreements will emerge, but they can be pretty sure that one side or the other is sure to read the agreement differently or want to make adjustments in light of changing circumstances.

Our panel assignment was simple enough: make the case for dispute prevention, not just facilitation or mediation. We were motivated by a simple cartoon showing someone peering down from the top of a cliff at a waiting ambulance below. The ambulance driver is ready to dash off to the hospital with the next victim injured in a fall; no one has thought to build a fence around the edge of the precipice to keep people from falling in the first place. We were talking about building a fence to avoid disaster, not just arranging to have an ambulance ready when the inevitable occurs.

It turns out that in the construction industry, dispute prevention has been the norm for years through the use of partnering agreements. Companies entering into construction contracts may have to work together for several years to complete a project. Delay at any point during the construction of a large building can kill a project. So, before construction begins, the financial sponsor, the architect, the builder, and sometimes others (like the construction union) sign an agreement, promising to meet regularly (whether there's trouble or not), keep lines of communication open, monitor progress jointly, and put a standing panel of neutrals (i.e., mediators or arbitrators—another kind of dispute resolver who is granted decision-making authority by the disputants) in place so that small disagreements can be resolved quickly, before they escalate. By putting a carefully designed dispute handling system in place, it turns out that most disagreements or misunderstandings can actually be avoided. There are unambiguous findings from numerous studies to support this.

Why, then, are dispute prevention measures so rare in other sectors? We speculated that it might be because industry leaders just don't know about the idea of partnering agreements or standing dispute resolution panels (which have very quick timetables for airing and resolving disagreements). But that seems unlikely since the same law firms and in-house counsel, trained at the same law schools, work in these other sectors too. So we explored other obstacles to using dispute prevention techniques. Our best guess is that law firms (or lawyers in general) might be the problem. What glory is there in being the person responsible for avoiding a dispute? And how can a legal services provider make any money if they succeed in avoiding most litigation?

I suggested that we add a provision calling for a dispute prevention bonus in all legal services contracts. So in fashioning a business deal, for example, the law firm involved in writing or reviewing the contract would add a provision calling for a financial bonus (set, perhaps, as a percentage of the expected value of the deal or the transaction) to be paid to the lawyers involved *if there is no litigation* throughout the life of the contract. Deductions from the total might be made to cover the cost of arbitration if the standing panel needs to use it (but not for rapid-fire mediation). Imagine all the lawyers working like crazy throughout the life of a project or a contract to be sure that parties stay in close contact, communicate effectively, smooth out their misunderstandings quickly, and take prearranged steps to resolve minor disagreements! I have no doubt that lawyers would become skilled in dispute avoidance if they had sufficient incentives to do so.

At the conference, we talked about the four prerequisites for dispute prevention. The first is a written dispute avoidance or dispute handling agreement that spells out appropriate procedures step-by-step. The second is a requirement that the most senior managers on both (or all) sides of a contract or a working relationship must be called in at the first sign of trouble. (This seems to motivate everyone below them to do whatever is necessary to keep things under control.) The third is the inclusion of a standing neutral or panel of neutrals, so that the parties don't have to scramble to find someone acceptable to

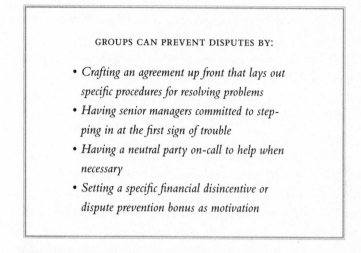

GROUPS CAN PREVENT DISPUTES BY:

- *Crafting an agreement up front that lays out specific procedures for resolving problems*
- *Having senior managers committed to stepping in at the first sign of trouble*
- *Having a neutral party on-call to help when necessary*
- *Setting a specific financial disincentive or dispute prevention bonus as motivation*

everyone—and who understands their business—when small problems arise. The last is an explicit financial disincentive or a dispute prevention bonus to keep everyone motivated.

My own take on dispute prevention is that clients of all kinds will have to demand that legal service providers emphasize the idea before it will spread as rapidly as it should.

WHAT TO DO WHEN THE OTHER PERSON IS LYING

THERE'S A LOT OF CONFUSION about the best way to respond to a lie. One strategy is to ignore it and act as if the statement was never made. People who take this tack hope they'll avoid giving a false statement any traction. A second strategy is to suggest that the person making the statement probably didn't realize what he or she was saying. This approach presumes that it's always best to give someone the benefit of the doubt and presume there's just a misunderstanding. I don't agree with either approach. From my standpoint, the most effective response to a lie is to name it, frame it, and claim it.

If I think someone is lying—that is, deliberating making a statement they know to be false, I'll say out loud, "That's a lie." Yes, I'm giving visibility to the statement, but from my standpoint, I'd rather the statement be labeled as a lie than allowed to stand unchallenged.

That's not enough. It is important to say why I think the statement is a lie and to suggest what the motive of the liar might be. I call this "framing." Motive is important. If I can't think of any reason the person might have for misrepresenting the truth, then I might chalk their statement up to ignorance or reckless disregard for the truth. So for me to call something a lie, I have to believe that the person making the statement has a motive for misrepresenting the truth. I link my characterization of their motive with the evidence that ought to convince any neutral observer that their statement is untrue. "That's a lie. That's not what it says on page 1,014. I can only assume you are trying to make the president look bad." Or, "No, that's not what happened on that date. I think they are saying that because they would rather have us believe something that casts them in a better light. Here's reliable information to the contrary."

Finally, it is important to own any claim that a statement is a lie. This means that I need to be comfortable making that claim. If I'm going to call someone a liar, I ought to do it in a very public way—to their face, if possible. I'm certainly not going to do it anonymously. The credibility of my characterization of their motive hinges, in part, on my willingness to stand behind my charge. "That's a lie. She is just trying to gain publicity for herself and play to her constituency. The bill doesn't say that at all. In fact, here's what it says. I'd love a chance to meet with her and have her show me exactly where it says what she claims."

Name it as a lie. Frame it by postulating the liar's motive and offering evidence to the contrary that any neutral observer would accept. And claim responsibility for your countercharge.

THE MOST EFFECTIVE RESPONSE

TO A LIE IS TO:

- *Name it*
- *Frame it*
- *Claim it*

PROVIDE LEADERSHIP
Build Your Organization's Negotiating Capabilities

THE RESPONSIBILITIES OF LEADERSHIP

THERE ARE A GREAT MANY theories of leadership—from highly centralized, top-down (almost militaristic) models to more decentralized, bottom-up, enabling (almost group self-management) models. Leaders who get others to do what they want by using their authority to threaten or punish can, in fact, get things done. As we flatten organizations, however, leaders who can get things done only by using strong-arm tactics are becoming obsolete. Organizations that have eliminated layers of middle management need lower-level staff to take more responsibility. In this context, companies and groups put a premium on finding managers who can motivate or catalyze networks of employees, volunteers, supporters, investors, and others to define what needs to be done, take the necessary initiative, and encourage cooperation.

I think of these people as "facilitative leaders"—men and women who help teams and networks of employees and partners set ambitious but workable agendas, solve problems in creative ways, and support each other and the organization as a whole in the face of unexpected opportunities and obstacles. Facilitative leaders foster the kind of empowerment that makes winning at win-win negotiation a reality. That is, your organization's leadership has to trust you to determine what it will take to get into the trading zone and win at win-win negotiation. They have to allow you the room to maneuver that you need in order to improvise. They have to support the choices you make along the way (with appropriate consultation). If you are the leader of an organization, you have to build the negotiating capacity of your organization, work to improve it, trust your negotiators, and reward those who succeed in winning at win-win negotiation.

From what we have learned in the consensus building and organizational development fields, I see three behaviors, or moves, that define facilitative leadership. First, a facilitative leader consults with the people she is leading in order to define the process by which the group will do its work or make decisions. Second, she finds ways to enhance the capacity of the individuals and groups involved so they have both the information and the confidence they need to make informed decisions or recommendations. It is not enough to invite people to have a say. A facilitative leader must give those being consulted access to the technical information or independent professional advice they need to develop their suggestions in meaningful ways. People being consulted also need to hear that their informal (local) knowledge is important and will be incorporated into whatever decisions are made. And third, she commits to decision making by consensus. That is, a facilitative leader won't impose a decision or settle for a majority vote; rather, she will keep working until the group comes as close as possible to unanimity about how to proceed.

A lot of leaders (including many of those who operate in a top-down fashion) claim that they want to consult or involve others in choices that must be made. But they don't mean it. What they really want is confirmation for what they have already decided or a veneer of democratic decision making. A facilitative leader, on the other hand, makes explicit what the process will be by which the input of all relevant parties will be tapped, presents that process for review and revision by the people who will be involved, and makes sure that the process is followed. Even facilitative leaders may have to impose time constraints or other limitations. But when they do, they make these constraints explicit along with their reasons for imposing them.

A commitment to consensus building often means involving a professional neutral to provide facilitation or mediation services, as I have described in earlier chapters. A facilitative leader knows that it is not a sign of weakness to ask for such help—especially when the leader wants to have a say on particular issues being discussed and thus isn't in a position to be entirely disinterested when engaging others in collaborative decision making. Consensus building also requires putting the right kinds of questions to the group—for example, asking for proposals that will solve a problem in a way that meets the

---

FACILITATIVE LEADERS:

- *Consult with the people they are leading to design an effective decision-making process*
- *Build the group's decision-making capacity*
- *Are committed to decision making by consensus*

interests of everyone involved rather than asking for each person's favorite solution. It also means insisting that the group shouldn't seek compromise but instead aim to maximize the creation of value—coming as close as possible to meeting the concerns of everyone involved.

It's hard to be a facilitative leader. It is certainly more of a challenge than being a traditional visionary leader who is supposed to figure out what's best and knock heads until everyone does what they are told. Here are some of the challenges of being a facilitative leader: You can't be present during every negotiation your organization has to complete. You have to empower your negotiators to improvise, at least as far as developing proposed packages or deals are concerned. And you need to build sufficient organizational negotiating capability so you can trust your individual negotiators to make good decisions on your organization's behalf.

We can see how a facilitative approach to leadership can be effective in the following situation, where framing crisis communication as a negotiation rather than as damage control may make it easier to win at win-win negotiation.

WHEN AN ANGRY PUBLIC WANTS TO BE HEARD

WHEN NEGOTIATORS GET ALONG WELL, creative problem solving is easy. When they become upset, however, they seem to forget everything they know about finding joint gains—they may even give up tangible wins simply to inflict losses on others. This is especially true in high-profile negotiations that turn nasty. Confronted with negative publicity, executives become so focused on controlling public relations and managing the crisis that they lose sight of the fact that they are in a negotiation.

Along with my colleague Patrick Field, I have looked at how corporate leaders and government agency directors react when confronted by consumers angry about an organization's past actions, future plans, or—worst of all—the values or objectives it represents. Examining real-life crises such as the *Exxon Valdez* oil spill, animal rights controversies, and the shutdown of Three Mile Island, we found that even the most experienced executives are prone to skip entirely the value-creating step in negotiations. In an effort to defend themselves or to lash out at those who are attacking them, many people in leadership positions fail to look out for their own best interests.

Some public relations experts argue that negotiations have no place in a crisis, to the relief of executives who dread the thought of having to confront those who are angry with them. Communication specialists have traditionally advised companies in such situations to focus on message control. Reveal as little as possible, they say. Deny liability. Avoid all forums that could legitimize your adversaries' views. Further, try to win the battle for public sympathy by denouncing your attackers' claims and hire experts or public figures to release favorable messages. When all else fails, prepare to buy off your opponents.

This advice ignores the fact that what an angry public wants most is to be heard. Experts in conflict management point out that if the only communication that occurs consists of both sides asserting their positions and demanding that the other side take certain actions, little progress will be made. Instead, try construing exchanges with angry parties as negotiations in which the primary goal is to search for tradeoffs that will lead to mutually beneficial outcomes. Even when agreement seems impossible, parties often can work together to create value. From our studies of past practices in industry and government, we have identified six prescriptions that we believe can help any organization facing an angry public win at win–win negotiation.

Acknowledge the Concerns of the Other Side

THIS CAN BE DIFFICULT TO DO, especially when lawyers worried about liability are involved. But organizations that take the time to acknowledge the concerns of others will often be able to avoid making large concessions. For instance, a company that wants to build a controversial factory, like Anaconda in chapter 1, might meet with angry abutters to acknowledge their concerns about possible adverse impacts. The company might also commit to ensuring that all relevant federal, state, and local regulations will be met if the factory is built.

Those who have been hurt by a corporation in the past (by an oil spill, for example) might begin their public campaign by demanding an apology. In many parts of the world, indigenous people involved in current disputes about the use of their land have opened negotiations by demanding apologies for hardship endured for generations. Typically, corporate executives and governmental officials react by denying personal responsibility for past events. A better strategy might be to express sympathy for the group's past struggles via a public statement that stops short of an apology. It is often possible to acknowledge the public's concerns without accepting responsibility and generating exposure to liability. This is another element of facilitative leadership.

Encourage Joint Fact-Finding

GENERATING MUTUAL GAINS in an emotionally heated situation often depends on developing a shared analysis or forecast. Without a common framework for analysis, it is too easy to fall into a test of wills. Unfortunately, embattled executives tend to seek expert or technical advice that will support their arguments and discredit their opponents. In such situations, as I described in earlier chapters, expert advisers tend to cancel each other out.

In disputes concerning human health and safety, it's important to bring reliable and unbiased data to the negotiating table. In the debate over genetically engineered foods, for example, scientists and environmentalists alike have presented self-serving arguments to the public about potential benefits and risks.

A better strategy would be for the groups to engage in joint fact-finding. You will remember that this process, as described in chapter 1, works as follows:

- Jointly choose a set of respected experts with different views and disciplinary backgrounds.
- Work with these experts to enumerate the scientific questions to be addressed.
- Allow the experts to articulate areas of consensus as well as disagreement.
- Question the experts on their analyses with the help of a neutral party.
- Ask the experts to interpret their findings in light of follow-up questions from the stakeholders.

This process does not turn decisions over to scientists or technicians, but it does ensure that the valuable information they have will be factored into the negotiation.

Offer Contingent Commitments

NO MATTER WHAT ANALYSIS the experts produce, a degree of uncertainty will always surround forecasts that lie at the heart of many controversies. Companies will argue that their plan will not have the ill effects that their adversaries predict, and their opponents will argue the opposite. After joint fact-finding has narrowed and grounded the dispute, the next step is to develop contingent commitments, as described in chapters 3 and 5, that will satisfy both sides. Contingent commitments are promises that will come into effect only if particular deadlines are missed or if performance standards are exceeded. If proponents believe that their plans truly are benign, they ought to be willing to commit to correcting any of the adverse consequences that their opponents fear.

In debates over land development, for example, abutters, like those living near the proposed plant in the Anaconda case, often fear that a project will decrease their property values. Developers might try to reassure residents by referring to commissioned studies. If the developers believe their own forecasts, they ought to be willing to offer the residents some equivalent of property value insurance. Once such a promise is in place, it no longer matters whose forecast is correct. Contingent commitments allow negotiations to move forward in the face of conflicting predictions about the future.

Accept Responsibility, Admit Mistakes, and Share Power

IN SOME CIRCUMSTANCES, only an admission of responsibility for past harm will clear the way for new agreements. One hospital in Florida, for example, faced an instance of medical malpractice over the death of a child. The child's heartsick family wanted to ensure that a similar tragedy would not befall anyone else. The changes they proposed could occur only if the hospital accepted responsibility for its errors and agreed to work with the child's parents and with other consumers to make procedural adjustments. After accepting responsibility in the case, the hospital leadership discovered that its overall liability decreased.

In our litigious society, legal advisers caution their clients against making any admission of error. Yet in many controversies, that is exactly what an angry public craves most of all. Injured parties need to feel that their plight has been acknowledged and that past mistakes will not be repeated. Only very strong leaders are willing to admit errors and take responsibility for mistakes.

Act in a Trustworthy Manner at All Times

THIS PIECE OF ADVICE may sound obvious, but when we look closely at what is involved in building trust, it is easy to see why it may be hard to follow. There are two fundamental rules for building trust: say what you mean, and mean what you say.

Of course acting in a trustworthy (though not necessarily trusting) fashion at all times becomes difficult when you're facing hostile adversaries. Lawyers and company spokespeople may press executives to try to put the best face on the situation. When trying to win over the other side, it can be tempting to sugarcoat bad news or make statements you're not sure are correct. But when others find out later that you exaggerated, shaded the truth, or dissembled, trust may never be repaired. Sometimes it's only after trust has been lost that executives at the center of a controversy realize what they've done wrong.

Focus on Building Long-Term Relationships

WHEN WE NEGOTIATE with the people closest to us, most of us try to give the other side the benefit of the doubt. We look for agreements that leave everyone better off, simply because we're concerned about the future of the relationship. By contrast, in our work lives, we have a greater tendency to view confrontations through the lens of a one-time situation. Most often, this focus is too narrow.

The fact is, most negotiations require parties to maintain decent working relationships, if only to ensure implementation of whatever agreements or understandings they reach. Problems are sure to crop up after agreements have been signed, and if the parties burned bridges during a negotiation, it may be difficult to fix them. In addition, a current negotiation may very well affect your reputation within the industry, or that of your company.

Thus, it makes sense to always negotiate as if the relationship matters. This may be difficult when there is bad blood between parties, but thinking ahead about the need to ensure that parties live up to their commitments is in everyone's self-interest.

Those six prescriptions for negotiating with an angry public rest on the premise that winning at win–win negotiation, even when the parties are seriously at odds, requires an effort to create value. Facilitative leaders understand this. After all, the larger the pie, the larger the pieces likely to be available to each stakeholder.

HELPING DECENTRALIZED ORGANIZATIONS NEGOTIATE MORE EFFECTIVELY

SUPPOSE YOU ARE THE MANAGER of a geographically dispersed organization with business units or key people spread out all over the world or across a large region. You might be part of a multinational corporation with offices in five or six countries; or part of the U.S. military with outposts in every corner of Afghanistan; or part of an international environmental NGO with branches in various parts of the globe. For the people in your organization to be able to negotiate effectively, they must be able to put their hands on information in a timely way, get reactions from other parts of the organization to proposals raised during negotiations, and find out all that they can about how your organization has handled similar negotiations in the past. These are all crucial to having the information and support required to propose winning packages, good for the other side and great for your side.

Networked communication is important to successful negotiation for at least three reasons. First, the experience of one node can be of great help to another node, especially if the lessons learned by one can be quickly and accurately shared with the others. Second, some negotiations undertaken by one node might hinge on the direct involvement of the other nodes. The sales staff in Europe, for example, might be negotiating a contract that they need the sales staff in Asia to be part of. Or the soldiers in a northern outpost, negotiating with a group they haven't interacted with before, may want to hear from other outposts that have negotiated with the same group elsewhere in the country. Or the African branch of a global NGO might be meeting with the subsidiary of a multinational that its European counterparts have dealt with before. Effective organizational negotiation depends on being able to tap past experience, build on lessons learned, and keep relevant organizational deadlines, goals, and protocols in mind. Third, possible deals often emerge during negotiation that were not considered beforehand. This means that permissions, or at least reactions, must be sought from other parts of the organization before a final commitment can be made.

Even with the recent accumulation of online tools, particularly those offered by social media sites, few if any organizations have networked negotiation support systems in place. There are, to be sure, software packages that individual negotiators can use to remind themselves how they should prepare for a negotiation or how to evaluate proposals that emerge during the give-and-take of an ongoing negotiation. But these are intended as instructional aids to help individuals negotiate more effectively; they are not designed to help decentralized organizations pull together everyone and everything that needs to be integrated.

Efforts are under way in many quarters to design specifications for an online negotiation support system to help decentralized organizations shore up their negotiating capabilities. Your organization should be thinking about its own online negotiation support system. Such a system should be really easy to use—as easy as Facebook. This means that once the system is in place, no one has to do any programming, although your users will undoubtedly want to customize the look and feel of the network. The system must be secure. When military leaders are using online negotiation support systems, they must be certain that no one is eavesdropping. So I am not talking about a traditional website, but rather something known as a "walled garden." Networked participants will probably need incentives (and clear instructions) from the top of your organization to encourage them to keep track of what's going on in important negotiations. And they'll need uncomplicated templates to use for their reporting—something as simple as a thumbs-up or thumbs-down icon applied to past negotiation practices would be nice. The results of past negotiations will have to be stored, tagged, and easily accessible to multiple users in your organization. I'm talking about a learning system that can adapt and generate new insights automatically as additional patterns emerge or as users think of new questions they want answered. The same system could support real-time coaching (more on this later in this chapter) as well as hot lines for anyone who needs emergency negotiation advice. Users will probably want quick access to a library of what your organization thinks of as best practices.

It is relatively easy to build an organizational learning platform that can do all these things. Begin by asking whether your company wants to improve its organizational (not just individual) negotiating capabilities. Next, figure out the kinds of negotiation information, advice, and assistance your staff needs. Have you documented stories about the obstacles your organization inadvertently puts in the way of its own negotiators? If not, you'll need to do this. To whatever extent your organization is decentralized, you can design an organizational learning platform that will make it easier for your managers and employees to win at win-win negotiation.

DON'T GET LOST IN TRANSLATION

AS THE BUSINESS WORLD becomes evermore global, the ability to skillfully navigate cross-cultural settings requires more and more attention. Organizational leaders must find ways to enhance the ability of their managers to work effectively in these settings. Even when negotiators on both sides of the table speak a common language, different cultural expectations can prevent messages from getting through. But with the right strategies, you can help your organization surmount cross-cultural barriers.

The evidence was building that there would be a significant market in Asia for the specialty office equipment produced by "Bullseye," an American company. Executives at Bullseye contacted several large retailers of office equipment in Japan and Korea. One of the Japanese companies responded positively and sent a representative to the United States for a meeting.

The Americans at Bullseye had compiled a thick report about their company and its products, and they put on a glitzy multimedia presentation. In contrast, the Japanese representative seemed unprepared. The lawyer for Bullseye pressed the Japanese representative for information about his company's structure and finances. Shrugging off the questions, the man turned to the Bullseye CEO and invited him to visit Japan.

"I could send one of our senior marketing people," the CEO responded.

This suggestion seemed to make the Japanese representative uncomfortable. "My president was looking forward to meeting you personally," he said. The CEO was not quite sure what to say.

Even with a common language and the best of intentions, negotiators from different cultures face special challenges. Had the negotiators on both sides of the table done their homework, they would have understood—and compensated for—these cultural differences:

- In Japan, a great deal of preparatory work is done behind the scenes, before contact is initiated. Had the American executives understood this, they would have found out much more about the Japanese company before the meeting, and they would not have showered the Japanese representative with information he likely already knew.

- In America, lawyers play a much more important role in business interactions than they do in Japan. Had the Japanese representative realized this, he would not have been so taken aback by the fact that the American company's lawyer took the lead in questioning.

- Japanese businesses often rely on intermediaries such as trusted financial advisers or business partners to make initial contact. If it turns out that a business relationship is inappropriate or unwanted, conversations can end with neither side losing face. Not knowing this, the Americans probably misconstrued the mandate of the Japanese representative, who was not authorized to negotiate or make decisions but only to see whether further conversation would be fruitful.

- Once a Japanese organization is ready to establish a business relationship, representatives at the highest level usually begin by making personal contact with their counterparts before discussing any details. This is why the Bullseye CEO's unwillingness to travel to meet the Japanese CEO was viewed by the Japanese representative as a lack of interest in exploring a business partnership and may have undermined any chance of the two companies ever striking a deal.

Trends in Cross-Cultural Advice

OVER THE PAST FEW DECADES negotiation analysts have suggested different strategies for surmounting barriers to cross-cultural negotiation. Not all of them have worked well. Here are sum-maries of these evolving strategies.

"To thine own self be true." The prevailing view in the late 1970s and early 1980s was that Americans seeking to make deals overseas should negotiate in their usual style and let others adapt. While this strategy may have encouraged potential business part-ners in other parts of the world to learn English, it did very little to enhance cross-cultural communication. As long as American negotiators pushed their own style and remained insensitive to their counterpart's culture, both sides remained confused by un-spoken intentions and the meaning of symbolic actions.

"When in Rome, do as the Romans do." It soon became clear that holding fast to one's traditional approach to negoti-ation in cross-cultural contexts would not help parties over-come serious communication obstacles. The result? A pendulum swing in the opposite direction. A strategy that gained popu-larity in the mid-1980s emphasized the need for Americans to learn more about the negotiation styles of other cultures. Amer-ican managers heading abroad to explore business opportunities, for instance, were encouraged to take seminars that introduced them to culturally appropriate communication techniques.

Unfortunately, this approach created new problems. For one thing, most people have trouble making a complete tran-sition to new ways of negotiating. Such transitioning entails a greater commitment of time and effort than busy executives are prepared to make. The non-American partner is likely to be baffled by the American's atypical negotiating style (adopted in an effort to be effective in the new circumstances) or to take advantage of the American's adaptation mistakes. In either case, the outcome is usually quite discouraging for the American negotiator.

Be sensitive to cultural differences. In the early 1990s the prescriptive advice from negotiation experts shifted yet again. Since then, Americans have been urged to be sensitive to cultural differences without sacrificing their own negotiating strengths. Many companies arm their new overseas staff with guidebooks outlining the do's and don'ts of local negotiation:

- Don't put your feet up on the table and show the bottoms of your shoes to your negotiating partners in the Middle East.
- Do haggle in certain parts of Latin America where unwillingness to do so would be misconstrued as a lack of interest in making a deal.
- In Japan, don't put off an invitation to socialize until after you've reached a deal.

Setting aside the question of whether cultural sensitivity is just another version of cultural stereotyping, this approach fails to account for the fact that some negotiating partners, due to their education or cosmopolitan background, are more likely to be insulted than comforted by such mechanical efforts at accommodation. Accordingly, these do's and don'ts should be applied on a case-by-case basis, rather than on a country-by-country basis.

In fact it may be that cultural norms are less of a significant factor in negotiation than we think. For a time during the 1980s, anthropologists tried to document specific cross-cultural negotiating barriers facing partners in international dyads (for example, Brazilians negotiating with Germans, Americans negotiating with Chinese, and so on). The effort failed when it became clear that the background, skills, style, and experience of each individual were more important than broad cultural tendencies.

Adding the Individual to the Equation

NONE OF THESE MAXIMS has proven to be a satisfactory approach to cross-cultural negotiation, in large part because they overlook the importance of individual differences. I recommend that you approach potential business partners not as cultural emissaries but as individuals with unique personalities and backgrounds. Try following these guidelines when preparing for talks with someone from a different culture.

Research your counterpart's background and experience. With a little homework, you should be able to learn about your negotiating partner's background and experience. If your counterpart has a great deal of international negotiating experience, you can probably assume that cultural stereotyping (and any effort to modify your negotiating strategy accordingly) is likely to create new communication difficulties rather than solve old ones. If you have trouble getting information about your negotiating partner, ask an intermediary with contacts at that firm or organization to make inquiries for you. (Be sure the intermediary understands that he is not authorized to make any commitments on your behalf.)

Enlist an adviser from your counterpart's culture. If you discover that the person with whom you are likely to be negotiating has little or no international or cross-cultural experience, consider enlisting someone from his culture to serve as your second during the negotiation. Rather than deferring to this adviser during talks, plan out signals in advance to indicate when you should take a break for additional advice. In this manner, your cultural guide can help you size up the situation, coach you as needed, and even interject if he feels you have made an egregious error or misinterpretation.

Pay close attention to unfolding negotiation dynamics. Listen carefully during talks. If you're unsatisfied with the answers you receive, reframe your questions and try again. If you're unsure about what the other side said, repeat what you think you heard. It's safe to assume that people living and working in different cultural settings often view or interpret the same events differently. But in our era of globalization, it's also true that we have more in common on the person-to-person level than you might expect. Don't ignore your intuition, and mind your manners.

Most business professionals recognize when they need technical or legal expertise to proceed with a deal-making interaction. Similarly, cross-cultural negotiators should realize

---

THINK OF YOUR NEGOTIATION PARTNER AS AN
INDIVIDUAL FIRST, NOT AS A CULTURAL EMISSARY:

- *Research your counterpart's background and experience*
- *Enlist an adviser from your counterpart's culture*
- *Pay close attention to unfolding negotiation dynamics*

that they might well need help sizing up the situation in advance, as well as interpreting the signals and norms that could make or break a negotiation in a cross-cultural context.

Communicating Across Language Barriers

WHEN NEGOTIATORS who don't share a native tongue enter into talks, they might rely on an interpreter or translator to make themselves understood. But are their meanings really getting across?

Researcher Raymond Cohen has examined the obstacles to negotiation created by semantic difficulties in translation. He cites the Sapir-Whorf hypothesis, which in its strongest form argues that language is a cognitive straitjacket that compels a certain way of constructing reality. An implication of this hypothesis, which was particularly influential in the 1950s, is that negotiators who speak different languages are limited not only by the language that they don't know but also by the language that they do know.

Subsequent linguistic research has challenged the more extreme versions of this hypothesis. Most linguists today accept that language both guides and somewhat constrains our perception and cognition, without fully determining them. The lesson for negotiators: language barriers can be surmounted with patience and care.

NEGOTIATING FOR CONTINUOUS IMPROVEMENT

YOU'VE FINALLY CLOSED THE DEAL. Months of travel and seemingly endless meetings have culminated in an agreement that you and your company can live with—though, admittedly, it's a little less than you had hoped for. You're eager to get back to your daily routine and put the exhausting experience behind you.

If you've ever felt this way, you're not alone. Managers involved in complex negotiations typically want nothing more than to turn their backs on the experience once it's over. Unfortunately, this tendency results in serious organizational losses because a great deal of negotiation experience is wasted.

Negotiation isn't a skill that can be acquired overnight. Rather, it requires constant refinement at the individual level and a strong commitment on the part of your organization. What can you do to make learning about negotiation a continuing process in your organization? I offer four suggestions: monitor and assess each manager's negotiation skills, use a negotiation preparation worksheet, provide ongoing negotiation coaching, and report the results of major negotiations—both good and bad—to your entire organization. These steps can help each manager take away appropriate lessons from each negotiation experience and leverage this knowledge for your company's or organization's benefit. Winning at win-win negotiation is not just a one-time concern.

Monitor and Assess Negotiation Skills

MANY ORGANIZATIONS SUBJECT their executives to rigorous performance reviews, yet few companies include negotiation effectiveness as one of the core competencies they track. Instead, negotiation is usually subsumed under categories such as "emotional intelligence," "interpersonal effectiveness," or "persuasiveness." The negotiator-related questions posed in most 360-degree assessments don't measure the right skills and abilities, such as preparation. When evaluators do assess negotiations, they typically rely only on post hoc accounts and overlook the details of the bargaining experience.

To accurately track improvements in a manager's negotiation capabilities, someone must monitor how that person is doing—before, during, and after several key negotiations. Before a negotiation begins, it's useful to review how well an executive prepared. Did she spend enough time thinking not only about her own interests but also about those of the other side? Did she clarify her organizational mandate, including her authority to make commitments? Did she identify options for mutual gain to be put on the table at the appropriate moment?

When it comes to assessing the negotiation itself, you should strive to find out how well the employee listened to the other side's concerns and how nimble she was in revising her sense of the other side's priorities in light of offers made. What kind of relationship did she build? How effective was she at creating value? Following the negotiation, did the manager coordinate adequately within the organization to ensure implementation of the agreement? Was she able to deal with surprises—changes in the business environment not covered in the agreement—when they occurred?

Even if a company ensures that its managers receive formal negotiation reviews and timely feedback, the more basic question of how to measure performance can be perplexing. Did the executive create enough value to warrant high marks for performance? Upper management should set explicit benchmarks internally before putting any performance system in place. Bristol-Myers Squibb, for example, not only instituted such benchmarks (spelling out milestones for particular high-value negotiations) but also offered senior managers the training they needed to assess the negotiation performance of their direct reports and to give them constructive criticism. The key: reward self-criticism, don't punish it. Negotiation performance reviews should help managers become their own best critics.

Use a Negotiation Preparation Worksheet

TO DETERMINE AT WHICH POINT they ought to walk away from the table in an upcoming negotiation, executives should check in with their back table beforehand. If senior managers are un-willing to invest time in such a conversation—or if they offer less-than-helpful advice, such as, "Whatever you do, don't lose that account!"—an executive can't be held responsible for poor negotiation preparation.

One solution is to use a negotiation preparation worksheet (see an example at the end of this section) that will engage the entire organization in the necessary preparation and can be used to gauge executive performance after the fact. A prepa-ration worksheet not only obligates a negotiator to account for all the factors that ought to be included in a negotiation strat-egy, but it also requires high-level sign-offs on all relevant es-timates. This provides a concrete basis for performance review once a negotiation is over; negotiators and their superiors can both check intentions against results.

Keep in mind that bonuses and other rewards should be linked not just to negotiation outcomes but to outcomes in light of initial expectations. That is, review agreements in light of the value created above and beyond the targets set in the preparation worksheet. It's too easy to be a Monday morning quarterback and judge every result as insufficient.

Offer Ongoing Negotiation Coaching

HOW CAN AN ORGANIZATION capitalize on its own negotiation experience? Through reflective practice: the process of considering the results of each negotiation in light of what the initial expectations were and then discussing what ought to be tried next. While each negotiator should take the initiative to reflect on her or his own practice, to truly learn from experience, most negotiators need continual coaching from mentors.

Negotiators and coaches should be carefully paired. Not every senior manager is cut out to be a negotiation coach, and not every coach will work well with all the managers who report to him. Ideally, senior managers would provide negotiation advice and feedback to all their direct reports. However, this is unlikely to occur for several reasons: senior managers are unlikely to make enough time available for this task; they may not be skilled coaches or negotiators themselves; and their direct reports are unlikely to be candid about their weaknesses. When past interactions have undermined trust, negotiators are likely to fear that a manager will hold the negotiators' self-evaluations against them.

For these reasons, I advise companies to establish an internal center where employees can receive ongoing negotiation advice and assistance. While only large companies like Hewlett-Packard have done this so far, there is no reason that any company couldn't do something similar on a smaller scale. The staff at such a center (which could be a single person) could help managers prepare for negotiation, offer analytic advice during ongoing negotiations, and review each negotiation once the results are in. The center staff could also track company trends and identify additional training or resources that might be helpful. They could locate and assign internal or external coaches to help negotiators facing consistent problems or challenges. Such a center should periodically report to upper management, identifying units that need help. For large companies, the return on investment in a negotiation center will pay off many times over in terms of company profitability. And even in a small company, the right advice in a single negotiation could mean the difference between a profit and a loss for the year.

Coaching won't work well unless everyone involved has a common framework. Without a shared negotiation vocabulary, managers will struggle to provide useful feedback on recent negotiations. Moreover, without a shared underlying theory of negotiation, employees are likely to disagree on the usefulness of prescriptive advice.

Coaching offers negotiators not only feedback and encouragement but also opportunities to experiment. If you made a mistake last time around, you can decide in advance to do something different the next time. Then you'll need to review the new results to determine whether you have improved. If these efforts aren't documented, it's easy to lose track of what can and should be learned. Each step requires a commitment of time and energy. Until it becomes an organizational norm, negotiation coaching is easily pushed aside when other pressing considerations arise.

Report Negotiation Results Internally

TO FURTHER IMPROVE NEGOTIATIONS, a few companies are considering publishing an internal negotiation newsletter that they will distribute on their secure company intranet. Each month, the person overseeing the newsletter will choose a negotiation completed by someone within the company. If they go forward with the idea, a business journalist will interview all the relevant individuals, including those outside the company, if they're willing. Using a consistent framework for analyzing the success of negotiations, the journalist will prepare a descriptive account of what happened, highlighting the strengths and weaknesses of the preparation that took place, assessing the face-to-face interactions, and tracking subsequent implementation efforts.

A regular negotiation newsletter would serve three purposes. First, it would put employees on notice that the company is interested in knowing how well all negotiations are being handled. Second, it would reinforce the key concepts and theory of negotiation that the company wants the staff to use in coaching and performance reviews. Third, it would force senior managers to spend some time thinking about negotiation, a practice that underscores the organization's commitment to coaching.

For a newsletter to work, a company must be willing to air its failures as well as its successes. This can be difficult to put

---

CONTINUALLY IMPROVE YOUR ORGANIZATION'S
NEGOTIATION CAPABILITIES BY:

- *Monitoring and assessing negotiation performance*
- *Using a Preparation Worksheet*
- *Offering ongoing coaching*
- *Reporting the results of major negotiations*

into practice, especially in a competitive environment in which everyone wants to be seen as a successful negotiator. Anyone selected for close scrutiny should be praised for their openness and willingness to contribute to the company's overall success, or the newsletter won't be worth the effort.

Negotiation Preparation Worksheet

DISTRIBUTE THIS WORKSHEET to everyone in your organization, and encourage anyone involved in an important negotiation to put in the preparation time necessary to answer the following questions.

- ☐ What authority do I/we have to make firm commitments in this upcoming negotiation?
- ☐ Who else needs to approve the analysis below?
- ☐ What are my/our interests in the upcoming negotiation?
- ☐ What are the other party's interests?
- ☐ What is my/our BATNA (best alternative to a negotiated agreement)?
- ☐ What is the other side's BATNA? If they have a strong BATNA, how might I/we raise doubts about how realistic they are being about their BATNA?
- ☐ What options/packages might I/we suggest for mutual gain that meet the other side's interests well and my/our interests very well?
- ☐ What arguments/criteria/reasons can I/we give for preferring the option/package that is best for me/us? How can I/we help the other side sell this option to their back table?

☐ What implementation problems are likely to arise if the other side accepts my/our proposal, and how might these be overcome?

Investing in Negotiation Training

THE HEAD OF HUMAN RESOURCES for a Fortune 500 company was responsible for ensuring that all 150 of the firm's top managers received negotiation training. After surveying her options, she hired one of the best-known training firms to offer an intensive two-day program on negotiation at four locations in the United States, Europe, and Asia. In addition to presenting their usual teaching package of readings, lectures, role-play exercises, and case studies, senior trainers added special features closely linked to the company's sales challenges. While the training process took six months from start to finish, the HR director felt it was worth the time and effort: 120 senior managers completed the course and gave it positive evaluations.

Two months after the program ended, the HR director received an e-mail from her company's CFO. After investing almost $350,000 in negotiation training, the CFO informed her, the firm had just failed to renew a key contract with a longtime client. "What evidence can you provide that the training was worth the price?" the CFO asked. The HR director had no idea how to reply.

US companies spend millions on negotiation training for their employees each year. Some organizations pay to send their employees to standard courses that draw participants from across the country, while others hire consultants to tailor courses to their organization's particular needs. After a one- or two-day session, managers go back to their jobs and, at least for a while, attempt to apply the negotiation skills they've learned.

The huge cost of negotiation training raises important questions. How much can the typical manager learn from a brief training course? How much value do standard and tailored programs add to an organization, and how can we measure that value? Which training approach is most likely to benefit which kinds of negotiators?

As it turns out, negotiation is as much an organizational task as it is an individual one, a point made above when I introduced the negotiation preparation worksheet. By changing companywide negotiation practices, managers can reinforce the good habits that employees acquire in training and encourage long-term innovation. Managers at all levels need clear guidance, however, on how to improve the return on investment in negotiation training. Here I provide an overview of the two basic types of negotiation training, discuss the goals of training as well as effective ways to assess results, and offer means of ensuring that the lessons learned in training will last. If you want to win at win-win negotiation, you must be able to count on your own organization to provide appropriate support at key moments, or at least not undermine your negotiating efforts. Negotiation training is one way to increase the odds that you will get the support you need.

Negotiation Training: Standard or Tailored?

CONSULTING FIRMS AND UNIVERSITIES offer short courses several times per year to an audience of midcareer professionals from all fields and sectors—public, private, not-for-profit. Should you go to one of these programs? Will it be worth the cost? Standard negotiation training incorporates exercises covering circumstances that all kinds of managers in a wide range of situations might encounter, such as salary or purchasing negotiations. You need only flip through a random in-flight magazine to get a sense of how omnipresent such negotiation training has become.

Some firms and schools also offer courses tailored to a company's or an organization's specific needs. They present intensive negotiation sessions designed for groups of midlevel or upper-level managers. Like standard programs, tailored programs cover basic negotiation theories and concepts, but they also include simulations matched to the challenges that specialized staff face on a regular basis.

In the 1950s, psychologist Kurt Lewin described effective adult learning as a three-step process: unfreezing old behavior through diagnostic exercises, framing new ways of thinking about problems through lectures and readings, and freezing new approaches by giving participants multiple opportunities to reflect on and try out new strategies. Does this match your own experience?

Whether standard or tailored, most negotiation training programs follow Lewin's basic model. They begin with a diagnostic—a simple two-party negotiation exercise. By comparing the outcomes of pairs of participants, trainers emphasize connections between particular negotiation strategies and outcomes. During the unfreezing process, participants often are shocked to discover how poorly they performed, typically by squandering long-term relationships in favor of short-term victories.

Reframing follows these exercises, as trainers present key principles for improving on-the-job outcomes. Subsequent exercises offer opportunities under fluctuating circumstances for participants to freeze freshly absorbed concepts and theories. In a no-risk, supportive training environment, participants are urged to raise questions about the sometimes awkward adjustments inherent in jettisoning their old approach to negotiation.

Drawing from the same body of theory as standard training, tailored programs highlight concepts that coincide with negotiation challenges confronting a particular group like yours.

The Goals of Training

WHAT ARE SOME REALISTIC GOALS for negotiation training? From an individual perspective, negotiation training can help you get better at sizing up negotiating situations, and it can jump-start the process of improving your performance. Unfortunately, the impact of negotiation training (as with training in other "soft skills," including communication, facilitation, and cultural sensitivity) is often short-lived. If you try to apply what you've learned during training, and you don't get the support you need (like on-going coaching), or you find that standard operating procedures in your company cut against what you have just been taught to do, you are likely to go back to whatever you were doing before that fit the setting you are in.

At the organizational level, training can help management benchmark the levels of negotiation skill already in place and highlight institutional obstacles to achieving better performance. Training sessions sometimes reveal the ways in which organizations impede success, such as limiting preparation time or inadvertently rewarding poor negotiating performance. One notable advantage of tailored negotiation training is that often it concludes with a discussion of how your organization can help you and other managers be better negotiators.

New ideas and skills acquired through negotiation training can add both immediate and long-term value to an organization. Better-trained negotiators can bring about improved short-term financial performance and also enhance long-term customer relationships, service delivery, and employee satisfaction.

Measuring Training Results

IN A PERFECT WORLD, negotiation training would almost always be a worthwhile enterprise. But in the real world of stretched-to-the-max budgets and overworked people, high-priced training programs sometimes appear to be a luxury. To what extent can you use the ideas and tools you've acquired in training to add value to your organization?

Unfortunately, many trainers fail to conduct even the most basic assessment of individual knowledge levels before and after training. Evaluations too often focus on atmospherics—Was the room comfortable? Did you like the trainers' presentation style? Could you see the screen?—hardly the probing questions needed to determine whether training achievements will stick. Even when trainers do take time at the end of a session to assess whether participants absorbed key concepts, it's too soon to say what value the organization might gain from its investment.

Here's the good news: researchers have come up with novel ways of gauging the success of negotiator training programs.

Measurement Strategies

DONALD KIRKPATRICK, professor emeritus at the University of Wisconsin, has created a four-level framework for measuring training outcomes, updated here by training evaluation experts Jack Phillips and Patricia Phillips with a fifth level.

Level I, Reaction: Was the training enjoyable? Was it useful?

Level II, Learning: If I test you on the concepts, will you know more than you did before the training?

Level III, Application: Do you know how to apply the training?

Level IV, Impact: What is the impact of training on important business or organizational outcomes?

Level V, Return on Investment: What is the ratio of direct and indirect costs of training to the benefits yielded from it?

Imagine the following situation. A fairly large American-based manufacturer is having trouble holding its market share for one of its best-selling products—a line of pricey household appliances. Less expensive knock-offs are flooding the market. The company decides to invest in a tailored training program for its worldwide sales staff. Since the company sells mostly to large retail outlets, the training focuses on a series of mock negotiating situations reflecting recent reports from salespeople who seem to be having a hard time maintaining current contracts at prevailing prices. The two-day training for more than eighty people went as expected and the participants gave the program a 13 rating on a scale of 15. Written comments suggest that the sales staff appreciated the clarity of the presentation and hoped the concepts introduced by the instructors would turn out to be useful. At the tail end of the session, however, during a final question-and-answer period, one of the more senior salespeople asked whether the company was going to give the sales staff more flexibility to make individual deals with big-name retailers, since that seemed to be a key lesson from the training. Sales staff needed to be more responsive to the concerns of each potential client. Winning in each sales negotiation required inventing different packages of trades. The trainer couldn't answer the question directly. None of the highest-level managers in the company attended the training, and the trainer did not have access to anyone with authority to grant such flexibility during the time she was preparing the course.

One way of assessing the helpfulness of a training like this is to use 360-degree evaluation. This asks individuals to assess their negotiation skill levels using a detailed online questionnaire before training begins. After training, all the participants are asked to evaluate their fellow trainees as well as their own progress. Questionnaire results show individuals how others perceive their abilities. Many participants are quite enthusiastic about the opportunity to measure their progress and learn how others rate them as negotiators. It's not clear, though, that 360-degree evaluations will get us from Kirkpatrick's Level II to Level III. And it certainly won't get us to Level IV.

Instead, I offer a three-step process that might get you to Levels IV and V. These steps will certainly provide senior managers with the data they need to evaluate their return on investment in training. Remember, directors and other senior managers should focus on the impact of training on organizational outcomes, not just on the individuals who participate.

How to Gauge the Value-Added of Negotiation Training

ASSESS THE VALUE that organizations can gain from negotiation programs, especially tailored courses, using these three steps.

Focus learning. At the beginning and end of training, trainers should notify participants that six to eight weeks after the program is completed they will receive a follow-up e-mail message requesting brief descriptions of at least two instances in which they intentionally used key ideas or methods presented during their negotiation training. Trainers have found that when participants are informed about this task in advance, and when their managers reinforce the message, they focus during training on skills they will try out at work.

Follow up on progress. Trainers send out the above-mentioned e-mail message, asking participants to respond with two short paragraphs describing their on-the-job efforts to apply what they learned. The trainers also ask for estimates of the savings or additional revenue their efforts generated for the company.

Report results. Whoever is tracking all of this compiles a report that not only describes individual achievements but also attempts to tally the overall financial savings or benefits generated by the entire group. Notably, I have found that the value reported in almost every instance totals at least ten times the cost of the training program.

TO ASSESS THE VALUE OF NEGOTIATION TRAINING:

- *Know the benefits of choosing a standard or tailored approach to training*
- *Clarify your goals beforehand*
- *Use strategic measurement strategies*
- *Follow up and test progress regularly*

Training can be a good investment for both individuals and companies, especially if it is keyed to building overall organizational negotiating capabilities.

THE IMPORTANCE OF GOOD NEGOTIATION COACHING

ALONG WITH WELL-DESIGNED TRAINING and the right kind of leadership, companies and organizations should take steps to ensure that all their negotiators, especially new arrivals and up-and-comers, get the feedback and coaching they need to improve.

Having been newly promoted to product manager, Terry was pleased when her boss told her that Joe, one of the company's top negotiators, would show her the ropes. With her first important negotiation looming, Terry met with Joe and asked for his advice on dealing with the client.

"Just be careful not to lose the account," he said. "And don't be a pushover."

"Right," Terry said. *Common sense*, she thought. "Maybe you could help me figure out our bottom line."

"Well, we obviously don't want to lose money on the deal."

"So, you're saying it's acceptable to just break even?"

"Listen," Joe sighed. "I'm sure you can work the numbers yourself. We wouldn't have hired you otherwise, right?"

Is this his idea of sage negotiation advice? Terry wondered as she left Joe's office.

Rather than building up her confidence, Joe had undermined it. Instead of giving useful advice, he had offered platitudes.

Many professionals have a knack for creating value, claiming value, and building great deals. Yet few are capable of helping others enhance their negotiation performance. Some offer weak advice that they themselves wouldn't follow. Many are oblivious to the qualities that make them effective negotiators, and thus are unable to share these traits.

As I mentioned earlier in this chapter, not everyone is cut out to be a negotiation coach. Yet an effective coach can be an invaluable asset, and such individuals most likely exist within your organization. In the remainder of this chapter, I'll provide a more detailed look at negotiation coaching and highlight the most important qualities to look for in a coach. After you have learned to distinguish good coaching from bad, you'll be ready to identify the best negotiation coach for you. Finding a good negotiation coach can be critical to winning at win-win negotiation. We all need help with reality testing. We all need someone who will be both sympathetic and critical. If we are setting out to get the other side to rethink its priorities and ask for a revised mandate from its back table, as I described in chapter 4, rehearsing possible ways of saying the relevant things is important.

What Is a Negotiation Coach?

ANYONE IN AN ORGANIZATION who can help teach others how to negotiate more effectively can become a negotiation coach. Coaching is best conducted one-on-one rather than in groups. Because few organizations formally promise ongoing negotiation training to their employees, most negotiation coaching is done off the books. And because the best negotiation advice will come from someone fully aware of the precise demands and constraints you're facing, look for a coach within your own organization who really understands what you are up against.

Rather than simply telling you what to do in a particular situation, effective coaches focus on improving your skills and helping you learn from your own experience. They are well versed in an explicit theory of negotiation that allows them to explain and predict what will and won't work in a consistent way. Effective negotiation coaches help you set goals, assist you in figuring out what techniques to try and what adjustments to make. They give you a chance to rehearse and they enable you to understand what happened after the fact. Specifically, good coaches give advice consistent with their own practice, stress the importance of preparation, help you rehearse new or awkward techniques, and debrief your final results.

A Good Coach Is Consistent

AS PART OF THE FIRM'S quarterly speaker series, Jane, a vice president, gives a presentation to the project managers on the topic of negotiation. She makes three main points: First, don't let the other side call the shots regarding the location, the agenda, and the parties present. Second, make a high opening bid in order to keep your bottom line hidden. Finally, don't squeeze the other side so hard that they lose their dignity. After the talk, one of the managers asks Jane for some help in sketching out an approach to an upcoming negotiation. Jane listens, then gives some suggestions that are quite different from what she said during the presentation. She largely contradicts the principles outlined in her talk because she knows that hard bargaining of that kind is likely to backfire. Why did she make those points in the first place? Because she thought other top managers might judge her to be weak if she suggested a mutual-gains approach to negotiation?

It's not uncommon for negotiation coaches to offer advice that's inconsistent with their own bargaining behavior. It is also not surprising that inconsistencies like Jane's can leave trainees confused about which practices to follow. This happens when coaches lack a clear theory of negotiation to back up their advice. When asked to make recommendations, they simply parrot tips they've heard from others or read in airline magazines. Only coaches whose practice is informed by a theory in which they fervently believe (and which has been vetted empirically) are capable of giving consistent negotiation advice.

Ideally, senior managers should be taught to identify potential discrepancies between their theories and their practice. But it's a rare company that allocates sufficient resources to address the disconnect between what negotiators say and what they do.

One simple way for organizations to improve consistency is to limit their pool of negotiation coaches. Not all senior managers should be expected to be able to give expert negotiation advice to their direct reports. Instead, organizations should identify and train a few senior managers who have real coaching talent and let it be known that they're available to give advice companywide. These individuals would learn to be explicit about the theory of negotiation they depend on to diagnose others' strengths and weaknesses (as well as their own).

Keep in mind that employees may be reluctant to ask for negotiation advice from their direct supervisors for fear of revealing weaknesses that could be held against them during performance reviews or salary discussions. For this reason, many trainees may actually prefer to get help from coaches in other parts of the organization.

A Good Coach Focuses on Preparation

DURING HIS LAST FEW NEGOTIATIONS, Brian has not done nearly as well as Tim, his boss, had hoped. All three contracts came in well below the margin the division expected. Tim, who signed off on each deal, is worried about taking heat from the new director of global purchasing, who has pressed every unit to reduce costs. As Brian's next negotiation approaches, Tim decides to show up unexpectedly and play "bad cop" to Brian's "good cop." Subtly, he'll show Brian how it's done—and help them both bring in a great deal.

As you might have guessed, Tim is making a number of mistakes as Brian's coach. Surprising Brian at an important negotiation is likely to rattle the already shaky negotiator. And the good cop/bad cop routine is not a sound strategy for creating value or winning at win-win negotiation. Most crucially, Tim has failed to help Brian prepare for the upcoming round of talks.

To see how the relationship between negotiation coach and trainee should work, let's consider another situation within the same company. Carmella, a unit manager, is concerned about how a new purchasing director's mandate will affect her upcoming talks with Naomi, the CEO of a consulting company central to Carmella's supply chain. Carmella has done business with Naomi for almost a decade and considers her a friend. Naomi has always delivered on time and on budget, and Carmella hasn't rebid the contract in six years. Now, the new purchasing director wants all contracts rebid.

Concerned about her dilemma Carmella approaches her company's CFO, someone who has given her helpful feedback over the years. Carmella explains the conflict between wanting to meet the purchasing chief's demands and not wanting to tell

Naomi that her contract will be rebid and might not be re-newed. The CFO listens at length and poses questions that help Carmella to think more clearly about her priorities. He asks Carmella to identify the other company's interests and to con-sider how Naomi's company might reduce costs. He also asks Carmella what she would expect from Naomi if the situation were reversed.

The discussion helps Carmella figure out how to approach Naomi and how to direct her own staff. It also gives Carmella half a dozen ideas about things she can say or do that will make it necessary for Naomi to reconsider the existing contract with her back table (within a framework of options that Carmella has produced).

What made the CFO a good negotiation coach in this sit-uation? He listened closely to the details and encouraged Car-mella to prepare for talks as thoroughly as possible. He also enhanced Carmella's likelihood of winning at win-win ne-gotiation by encouraging her to get Naomi to go back to her back table with new options that are good for Carmella and her company, as well as for Naomi and her company.

A Good Coach Rehearses and Debriefs

DANNY ALWAYS GETS RESULTS. His division at one of the coun-try's largest investment firms has topped the charts for five years running, far surpassing the profitability of the firm's other re-gional units. But a reorganization looms. A shift to a matrix model (along the same lines as Wall Street Associates faced in chapter 2) will require Danny to report to a product manager in addition to his usual regional account manager. How can he please both managers, win a large bonus, and still get great results? Danny knows it's time to see his mentor—the guy at the top who has always given him strong advice.

Over lunch with Ralph, Danny explains the problem. "How am I supposed to negotiate expectations with my new boss and stay on good terms with the old one?" he asks.

"Offhand, I'm not sure," Ralph says. "Let's talk it through."

They start by role-playing the conversation Danny might have with the new product manager. Next, they rehearse Danny's talk with his long-term manager. Ralph, who has been at the front lines of the "reorg wars" for nearly two decades, does a great job of playing both parts. He also encourages Danny to take the risk of being a bit more outspoken in voicing his concerns about the restructuring.

Danny leaves the lunch with renewed confidence. Initial discussions with both of his bosses go well, and he schedules a celebratory drink with Ralph.

After toasting Danny's apparent success, Ralph urges him to question whether he made any mistakes in one or both of the meetings. Together, they cover what Danny might have done differently, as well as tactics he might try in future negotiations. By carefully balancing criticism with support and grounding his advice in tried-and-true theories, Ralph helped Danny strengthen his negotiation skills as well as his position within the firm.

A "Good Coach" Checklist

WHAT QUALITIES SHOULD YOU FOCUS ON when evaluating a potential negotiation coach? Effective coaches:

- Help you set your own goals rather than telling you what your goals should be.
- Encourage you to try new tactics and take risks.
- Offer support while leading you to confront what went wrong and why.
- Ask questions that enable you to figure out what you can learn from your experience.
- Model advice in their own practice.
- Honestly and humbly share their own negotiation experiences, positive and negative.

It is difficult to get a negotiating partner, whether internal or external, to rethink their mandate or return to their back table seeking clarification of their organization's options or interests. But getting them to do so is usually necessary if one is to win at win-win negotiation. You've got to be able to create more value (by getting the other side to consider options or packages that are good for them and great for you). If they have no room to maneuver—because they have been instructed to read the same script over and over again, no matter what new information comes to light or what counterproposals have been offered—it is very hard to create value. Unless you can create more value, claiming a significant share of the value available is exceedingly difficult. We all need a coach we can turn to in such situations, someone who understands what's going on, someone sympathetic to our interests, someone who will give us the criticism and support we need to test possible strategies for getting our counterparts to ask for different advice from their back table.

THE BEST COACHES ARE CONSISTENT AND
KNOWLEDGEABLE, AND THEY FOCUS ON:

- *Preparation*
- *Rehearsing what you are going to say
  to the other side*
- *Helping you learn from your experience*

CODA

Finding the Sweet Spot in Your Next Negotiation

WINNING AT WIN-WIN NEGOTIATION means being able to handle the claiming problem. You now have six strategies that should make that easier, even when you are dealing with difficult negotiators or negotiating situations. In every instance, you've got to get the opening right so that you can move as quickly as possible into the trading zone. Then you need to invest heavily in value creation, avoid compromise, and convince yourself to aim for your sweet spot—that point on the win-lose continuum where you are as far above your minimally acceptable outcome as you can get and the other side is sufficiently above theirs to claim victory when they report to their back table.

Get the Opening Right and Find Your Way into the Trading Zone as Quickly as Possible

MOST NEGOTIATORS START OUT thinking they know what they want. That is, they know their aspirations. They also believe they have a pretty good idea of what the other side wants. Many do not, however, spend enough time assessing or trying to improve their walk-away. They don't spend nearly enough time trying to estimate their negotiating counterparts' walk-away or the ways they might raise doubts about how favorable the other side's walk-away really is. Too many negotiators spend too much time repeating their initial demands and pushing their own objectives—often exaggerating what they "must have"—and fail to probe carefully what the other side wants (their aspirations) and needs. This makes it difficult to find the trading zone.

At some point, almost every negotiator must reassess his initial strategy by asking himself, "Will I get something better than my minimum walk-away if I keep pushing my initial demands? If I don't find a way to help the other side meet what I now understand to be their most important concerns, will I be able to get them to agree to anything?" Many negotiators get locked into an unreasonable opening or preemptive demands. They fail to make adjustments. The most successful negotiators, on the other hand, revise their objectives and strategy based on what they learn by asking good questions. Most importantly, they have confidence in their ability to improvise.

Often, negotiator rigidity is caused by the misplaced concern, "If I drop my opening demands, the other side will think I am weak." Yet, it's not rational to stick to demands that you know the other side cannot possibly accept. Some negotiators convince themselves the other side is bluffing when they say they can't accept an opening offer. So they just keep hammering away. Or they are locked into unworkable promises they made to their back table before they started; they are not empowered to make adjustments. Getting into the trading zone requires flexibility, the ability to ask good questions, and a mandate from one's back table that encourages improvisation.

Many people are not conscious enough of timing. They intentionally open with an overly ambitious demand, intending to make gradual concessions until they reach a final point that is still above their minimally acceptable outcome. This is the gist of hard bargaining. Unfortunately, such concession trading can backfire. Sometimes the other side will just walk away, insulted, when they hear an opening demand that is hopelessly out of bounds. They won't wait for another round of concessions; they will just assume that there is no chance of finding the trading zone and break off negotiations. So one side's intent to go slowly may conflict with the other side's quick estimate that agreement is not possible.

If everyone were completely open about their priorities or interests at the outset, and felt comfortable talking honestly about the tradeoffs they were willing to consider (and why), they could move quickly into the trading zone. They might, however, discover that there is no deal space. In my view, that wouldn't be a bad thing. It would avoid useless conversation. In fact, experienced negotiators don't waste time bluffing or trying to psych each other out. They move into the trading zone as quickly as they can, or move on to the next negotiation.

In every situation the deal space, if there is one, is bounded by walk-aways or BATNAs—on both (or all) sides. For example, if I have an offer from your competitor in my pocket when we start negotiating, that's my BATNA. If you don't match it or offer me more, I will walk away. Other times, it's not so easy to estimate my walk-away. If I'm a salesperson and I have a potential buyer for my product, but they insist on a discount, I may have no way to know whether someone else will come along quickly enough to buy my product (without demanding a discount) so I can meet my monthly sales quota. In that case, it is unclear whether I should walk away or not. In either situation, the deal space is the distance between our BATNAs or our realistic walk-aways. If that space is large, each of us will want to be at the edge of the continuum where our costs are lowest and the benefits to us are highest.

When we are in the deal space, we are in the trading zone. While it has real boundaries, the trading zone is also a state of mind. We're in it because we are optimistic about reaching agreement. When we ask constructive questions—and don't just present arguments on our own behalf—and we explore each other's interests, we probably have found our way into the trading zone. But when we keep repeating opening demands and arguing on behalf of what we want, we are probably not there.

Here's how this looks analytically:

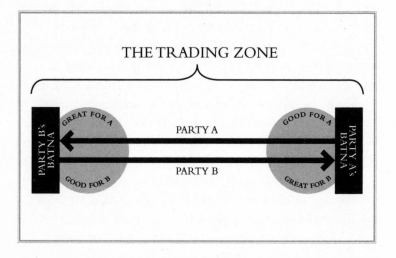

To discover the actual boundaries of the trading zone, try to use what-if questions. "If I offer you X, would you give me Y?" Linked offers of this kind, especially a series of such questions, help to reveal the boundaries of the deal space.

Invest Heavily in Value Creation

CONSIDER THE FOLLOWING EXAMPLE. A big company, "Mammoth," wants to expand into a new territory. A small competitor company, "Tiny," already controls the area. Mammoth wants to buy out Tiny so it will have clear sailing in the new market. The leaders of the two companies meet to discuss a buyout. They have both done their homework and have data to support their claims about what they think the value of the deal should be. Mammoth points out that it could put Tiny out of business entirely, so the buyout price should be low; accordingly, it makes a low-ball offer. Tiny counters with the claim that it has other suitors who have offered a lot more than Mammoth. Maybe that's true and maybe it's not. Tiny throws out a startlingly high number. They are stuck, so they decide to take a break.

During an informal moment, everything takes a new turn. The negotiator for Mammoth discovers that Tiny has been thinking about shifting its product line in a way that Mammoth never thought of and could not possibly replicate on its own in the near term. Suddenly, it occurs to Mammoth that a partnership rather than a buy-out would make more sense. Mammoth could build on Tiny's understanding of and reputation in the new area. Tiny will happily take a fair price for not competing with Mammoth. This will provide the money it needs to underwrite the retooling required to shift to its new product line. (Tiny has been having trouble finding capital.) By combining their efforts, they can sell both Mammoth's traditional product and Tiny's new product into the market more effectively than either can manage on its own. They can share marketing and distribution costs. While there are a lot of details to work out, a partnership rather than a buyout now seems more advantageous.

Were you able to recognize the moment they moved into the trading zone? It happened when they both saw the chance to create value: when they discovered that (1) the two sides' interests were interlocking, not opposed; (2) they would both be better off if they avoided an all-out battle over price that would undermine their relationship and make it harder to work together; and (3) there were deal options neither of them imagined before the negotiations began. In short, it was when they discovered reasons to be optimistic about finding mutually advantageous trades, since both had the authority to improvise in the trading zone. Once they explore those trades, the outlines of the deal space will become apparent.

What If the Parties Haven't Done Their Homework or Aren't Authorized to Make a Reasonable Deal?

IT'S HARD TO CREATE VALUE or to know if you are in the trading zone if one or both sides won't play the What-If Game. Sometimes this occurs because the parties haven't done their homework. They are prepared only to present their initial demands. They haven't thought carefully about their interests or their organization's interests. Other times, negotiators are given a highly restricted mandate by their back table and are not authorized to explore possible trades or improvise in any way.

The best example of this problem I know concerns delegates who represent nations in global treaty negotiations. Each national representative spends months working with different political actors inside their country to clarify what they are going to say at a scheduled global negotiating session. Before they go, they have to decide what they will stress and what they are willing to sacrifice during multicountry negotiations. When they are finally sitting across the table from all the other negotiators in a big assembly hall, they read the script they were authorized to present before they left home. It doesn't matter if their formal statement ignores what every previous speaker has had to say. All they can do is read their prepared remarks. Indeed, that's exactly what happens. Each negotiator plays primarily to his or her home crowd. Any deviation from the prepared script would probably result in their being called home and reprimanded.

At night, at the bar, when negotiators chat informally and everyone can speak off the record, that's when possible trades get discussed, and when there's a chance of finding the trading zone. At the end of several weeks of formal negotiating, the chair of the session usually distributes a revised version of the proposed treaty. This may be quite different from the draft each country spent so much time reviewing before their representative left for the meeting. Typically, the new version of the treaty is the result of trades that emerged at the last minute. No one, except the chair, is likely to take credit publically for the new package because most of the negotiators did not have authority to propose anything other than what was agreed to internally before they left. Unfortunately, the early draft of the proposed treaty was all they had to consider when they prepared their opening remarks and hammered out their country's negotiating stand. When the revised treaty suddenly emerges, each negotiator must call home. (In each country, "home" is represented by a different political leader, agency, or cast of characters.) During that last-minute call, each country must make a choice. "Do we support the revised treaty that the chair has distributed at the last minute? Yes, or no?" Further discussions, or still other trades, are not possible because everyone has a return flight scheduled in a few hours.

Think of the poor negotiators who didn't do their homework ahead of time, or were given no room to maneuver by their back table. They had no impact on the final outcome because they were not empowered to participate in informal trading sessions. All they could do was repeat their opening demands. Ideally, a negotiator needs to know what his or her country's most important interests are (and which of many ways of meeting those interests might be acceptable). On top of that, negotiators need a clear mandate indicating what they should say at the outset, what new options they can invent, and what package or trades they can support. Until the final moment, negotiators need to be able to explore what-ifs of all kinds. When the chair produces the final version of the treaty, each negotiator only gets to say yes or no. At that point, they must assure their back table that their most important interests will be met.

Avoid Compromise

I WANT TO BE ABSOLUTELY CLEAR that when I talk about trades, I am not talking about making concessions or compromising. Only through the exploration of possible trades can we discover whether there is a deal space and what its boundaries might be. We can do this effectively only if we employ a rapid sequence of what-if questions rather than opening with exaggerated demands followed by an exchange of concessions.

No negotiating party should ever accept an agreement that is worse for them than no agreement. When I hear the word "compromise," that's what I think of—terribly sub-optimal deals. In my view, one or both sides taking less than their walk-away, just for the sake of reaching agreement, is always a bad idea. For me, "compromise" involves accepting a package that is worse than your BATNA. I realize there are situations where it is difficult to predict what will happen if there is no agreement, so rather than walk away, parties accept something rather than nothing. Being unclear at the outset about when to walk away can lead to such sub-optimal deals. I also know that parties are often unsure what to do when their personal interests are at odds with the mandate they have received from their back table. For instance, a longtime country negotiator, ready to retire, wants some kind of agreement, even a poor agreement, to show for all his years of effort. Should he accept a weak deal (from his back table's perspective) if it meets his personal interests?

Some negotiators are not sure they know what their walk-away is at the beginning of a negotiation. Either they haven't done their homework, or their organization hasn't given them the information they need. During the back-and-forth, as the negotiation unfolds, they may realize that their walk-away options aren't as good as they imagined. This might cause them to accept a deal that others, who did not participate in the give-and-take, would see as a weak compromise. Nevertheless, I would stand by my claim that parties should not accept a deal that is worse for them than their walk-away as best they understand it. Sometimes it may be necessary to take a break during an ongoing negotiation, just to reassess one's walk-away, or even to take parallel steps to generate some other walk-away options.

In some circumstances, parties may not be sure whether they should walk away or not. "If we don't reach agreement now, I'm not confident I know what will happen next. Maybe I'm better off accepting the agreement that's on the table, rather than no agreement at all." Or they might say yes to something that turns out to be much less desirable than they imagined it would be. Nevertheless, in my view, no negotiator should knowingly agree to something that hurts their side more than no agreement would. Certainly they should not accept a weak agreement in an effort to encourage or curry favor with a negotiating partner. And they should never settle for a compromise just to justify the time and effort they invested (this is known as "too much invested to quit"). Agreements should reflect a hardheaded assessment of what the outcome represents for your side. Moreover, good working relationships (and particularly trust) are not achieved by caving in to pressure or agreeing to a lopsided deal. Rather, they are the by-product of all sides acting in a principled way. As Roger Fisher, William Ury, and Bruce Patton so elegantly explain in *Getting to Yes: Negotiating Agreement without Giving In*, negotiators should not give away their interests in the hope of buying a good relationship. All that does is teach the other side to expect more of the same self-defeating behavior in the future.

Some negotiators are in a big rush to get things done. Remember my story about buying the cottage at Golden Pond? As soon as the outlines of a plausible agreement emerged, I pushed too quickly to close the deal. While I didn't want to disappoint my wife, I probably could have paid less. Until negotiators have worked as hard as they can to create as much value as possible—even if one side is carrying most of the burden of doing this—it is not a good idea to accept a sub-optimal agreement (i.e., one that leaves both sides barely above their walk-aways) before exhausting all value-creating or trading possibilities.

Finding Your Sweet Spot

ONCE CLAIMING BEGINS, cooperation gives way to competition. There's no way to avoid it. The good news is that once you are in a deal space—in the trading zone—both sides are guaranteed a better outcome than if they walked away. The bad news is you have to figure out how to divide the value you have created.

An all-out battle is likely to lead to hard feelings. Purely competitive behavior can undermine even long-standing relationships. On the other hand, there is no way to avoid the tension that arises when claiming begins. Many negotiation analysts urge parties to talk directly about how to distribute value. I agree, but this is not enough. It implies that a compelling justification for a proposed split will carry the day. Yet one side will argue that an even split makes the most sense, marshaling relevant precedents to back up that assertion. The other will counter with the claim that they brought the most (e.g., capital, ideas, or connections) to the table, so they should get a disproportionate share. Both will work hard to emphasize nonemotional, or factual, arguments that any independent observer would accept as true. Nevertheless, this will not solve the problem. There is no correct solution to the claiming problem.

To justify your claims, you must be able to write the other side's victory speech. They have to be able to hold their head up when they explain to their back table why they got the share of the value they did. In short, you have to be able to help the other side deal with their back table's expectations.

Look again at the trading zone diagram.

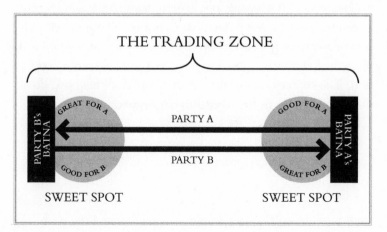

THE TRADING ZONE

PARTY B's BATNA

GREAT FOR A

PARTY A

GOOD FOR A

PARTY A's BATNA

GOOD FOR B

PARTY B

GREAT FOR B

SWEET SPOT

SWEET SPOT

This time, note the location of the two sweet spots (in gray)—yours and theirs. One is better for you and one is better for them. Why shouldn't you seek to end up in your sweet spot rather than theirs? In my view, this is a psychological question more than an analytical one. Can you convince yourself it is OK to end up in your sweet spot? What will it take to give you sufficient confidence to engage in such claiming behavior? *As long as you know you have done everything you can to help your negotiating counterpart get more than their minimum walk-away (by working hard to create as much value as possible), and you can write a plausible victory speech for their back table, you should feel comfortable aiming for your sweet spot.* My colleague, Bob Mnookin, talks about this in terms of empathy versus assertiveness. If you are too empathetic and not assertive enough, you won't reach your sweet spot. If you are too assertive and not sufficiently empathetic, you'll probably get no deal at all.

You must give your counterpart a way to show their back table they have been successful. It is your responsibility to spell this out. Even though a mutual-gains or a win-win approach to negotiation requires empathy and self-interested cooperation (to create value), winning at win-win negotiation also requires a commitment to assertiveness or claiming. The point of win-win negotiation is not to make friends, it is to get a good deal, maintain or improve relationships, and enhance your reputation. The six moves described in this book will help you do all these things even in the most difficult negotiating situations.

ACKNOWLEDGMENTS

SOME OF THE MATERIAL in this book first appeared in *Negotiation*, a monthly newsletter published by the Program on Negotiation at Harvard Law School. Many thanks to Katie Shonk, editor of *Negotiation*, for all the improvements she made in those early articles. Thanks also to Carri Hulet at CBI (Consensus Building Institute), who did an amazing job organizing and editing the initial version of this volume. My agent, Jim Levine, of the Levine-Greenberg Company, ensured publication of this book—thanks, Jim. John Mahaney, of PublicAffairs, provided crucial editorial advice and tireless assistance. I greatly appreciate the help of everyone at PublicAffairs/Perseus.

Many thanks to the Program on Negotiation at Harvard Law School for permission to excerpt and reprint in modified form:

"When an Angry Public Wants to Be Heard: Approaching Crisis Communications as a Negotiation Rather Than as Damage Control May Save the Day," November 2003
"First, Find the Facts: When Negotiators Are Squaring Off over a Contentious Issue, Joint Fact-Finding Can Get Talks Off to the Right Start," December 2003
"Winning and Blocking Coalitions: Bring Both to a Crowded Table:

In a Multiparty Negotiation, You Need a Good Offense to Forward Your Interests and a Good Defense to Thwart Others' Aggressive Moves. Coalitions Can Provide Both," January 2004

"When You Shouldn't Go It Alone: Recognizing When You're in Over Your Head and Need an Agent Can Help You Come Out on Top in a Negotiation," March 2004

"Divided, You'll Fall: Managing Conflict within the Ranks: Flatter, Matrixed Organizations Require an Integrated Approach to Managing Conflict," June 2004

"Negotiation Training: Are You Getting Your Money's Worth? Companies Can Send Employees to the Best Courses Yet Still Not See Positive Results. Here's Why This Happens—and How to Fix It," August 2004

"What Gets Lost in Translation: Even When Negotiators on Both Sides of the Table Speak a Common Language, Different Cultural Expectations Can Prevent Messages from Getting Through. But with the Right Strategies, You Can Surmount Cross-Cultural Barriers in Negotiation," September 2004

"Stubborn or Irrational? How to Cope with a Difficult Negotiating Partner," Dec 2004

"Don't Like Surprises? Hedge Your Bets with Contingent Agreements: No One Can Predict the Future. But You Can Protect Your Accord by Using Contingent Agreements That Anticipate Potential Changes," January 2005

"Handle with Care: Negotiating Strategic Alliances: How to Adjust Your Approach When Bargaining with a Partner Who's Key to Your Strategy," April 2005

"Breaking Robert's Rules: Consensus-Building Techniques for Group Decision Making: Deciding by Majority Rule Puts a Premium on 'Winning' Rather Than on Producing the Best Possible Outcome for Everyone. An Alternative Approach Can Achieve a Decision That Is Closer to Unanimous," May 2005

"Full Engagement: Learning the Most from Negotiation Simulations: How to Acquire Real Negotiating Skill—without Risking Real Consequences," August 2005

"Negotiating with Regulators: Securing Licenses and Permits Can Be Daunting. Here's How to Improve Your Odds of Success," November 2005

"Negotiating with a 900-pound Gorilla: Faced with Taking the Other Side's Offer or Being Squeezed out of the Market? Here's How to Expand Your Options," February 2006

"What's Special About Technology Negotiations: High-Tech Negotiations Present Particular Challenges. Here Are Three Steps to Take to Surmount Them," May 2006

"Negotiating for Continuous Improvement: How to Help Your Managers—and Your Company—Learn from Each Negotiating Experience," June 2006

"Bring Talks Back on Track with Facilitation. When Tempers Flare and Anarchy Threatens, an Outside Expert Can Increase the Productivity of Group Negotiations," September 2006

"Think Fast! Expect the Unexpected at the Bargaining Table. Practice the Element of Surprise and Turn Moments of Panic into Opportunities for Value Creation," November 2006

"Find More Value at the Bargaining Table. Many Professionals Are Too Quick to Give Up the Search for Better Outcomes for All Sides. Improve Your Deal's Quality by Mastering These Four Value-Creating Moves," February 2007

"Finding a Good Negotiation Coach. Not All Successful Negotiators Are Cut Out to Be Coaches. Here's How to Select the Right Person to Help You Improve Your Bargaining Skills," August 2007

"How to Negotiate When Values are at Stake. Negotiators Are Accustomed to Focusing on Interests. But to Resolve an Entrenched Dispute Over Differences in Values and Beliefs, You'll Need a New Set of Tools," October 2010

NOTES

The following materials were either cited directly or offer additional ideas about the topics covered in each chapter.

INTRODUCTION: FINDING THE TRADING ZONE AT GOLDEN POND
The shift from win-lose to win-win in the public mind was marked by the publication of Roger Fisher, William Ury, and Bruce Patton, *Getting to YES: Negotiating Agreement without Giving In* (Penguin, 1991).

In James Sebenius and David Lax, *3-D Negotiation: Powerful Tools to Change the Game in Your Most Important Deals* (Harvard Business Press, 2006), additional dimensions of negotiation are introduced.

Robert Mnookin et. al., *Beyond Winning: Negotiating to Create Value in Deals and Disputes* (Belknap, 2000), extends and enhances the discussion that Fisher, Ury, and Patten began, focusing especially on legal negotiations.

Another shift in the negotiation field is about to begin with the publication of Michael Wheeler, *The Art of Negotiation: How to Improvise Agreement in a Chaotic World* (Simon and Shuster, 2013). The importance of improvisation as a negotiation skill is clearly established by Wheeler.

The concept of predictable surprises was first noted by Max Bazerman and Michael Watkins in *Predictable Surprises: The Disasters You Should Have Seen Coming, and How to Prevent Them* (Harvard Business Press, 2008)

SIX WAYS OF WINNING AT WIN-WIN NEGOTIATION

**CHAPTER 1. LEAD THEM INTO THE TRADING ZONE: HELP YOUR
NEGOTIATING PARTNERS REFRAME THEIR MANDATE AND PRIORITIES**
Dealing with Stubborn or Irrational Partners
The most important description of rational negotiating behavior is pro-
vided by Max Bazerman in *Judgment in Managerial Decision Making* (Wi-
ley, 2005), and Max Bazerman and Margaret Neal, *Negotiating Rationally*
(Free Press, 1994). These books summarize the psychological biases or
traps that even the most rational negotiators fall into.

First, Find the Facts
The idea of the trading zone originated with Peter Galison, *Image and
Logic: A Material Culture of Microphysics* (University of Chicago Press,
1997), and was expanded upon by Boyd Fuller in his 2006 MIT doctoral
dissertation, *Trading Zones: Cooperating for Water Resources and Ecosystem
Management When Stakeholders Have Apparently Irreconcilable Differences.*

The process of joint fact-finding is described in detail in Lawrence
Susskind, Sarah McKearnan, and Jennifer Thomas-Larmer, *Consensus
Building Handbook* (Sage, 1999)

How joint fact-finding fits into the larger process of mediation, or
joint problem-solving, is discussed in Lawrence Susskind and Jeffrey
Cruikshank, *Breaking the Impasse: Consensual Approaches to Resolving Public
Disputes* (Basic Books, 1987).

Practical examples of how joint fact-finding works are provided in
Lawrence Susskind and Jeffrey Cruikshank, *Breaking Robert's Rules of Or-
der: The New Way to Run Your Meeting, Build Consensus and Get Results*
(Oxford University Press, 2006).

Negotiating with a 900-Pound Gorilla
Power asymmetries in negotiation are analyzed quite elegantly in Roger
Fisher's article "Negotiating Power: Getting and Using Influence," *The
American Behavioral Scientist* 27, no. 2 (November 1983): 149–166.

For a more complete discussion of the role that coalitions play in
negotiation, see Lawrence Susskind and Larry Crump, *Multiparty Negotiations,* 4 volumes (Sage, 2009), especially the introduction to volume 1.

Overcoming the Not-in-My-Backyard Syndrome
The most compelling explanation about the rise of NIMBYism is presented in Michael O'Hare, Lawrence Bacow, and Deborah Sanderson, *Facility Siting and Public Opposition* (Van Nostrand/Reinhold, 1983).

More than twenty years ago, my colleagues and I at MIT figured out how to overcome the NIMBY syndrome and crafted what we called "The Facility Siting Credo" (Lawrence Susskind and Howard Kunreuther, *Negotiation Journal 6*, no. 4 [October 1990]]: 309–314). The Credo was tested nationally against the siting experience in a great many American cities. The results are described in Howard Kunreuther, Kevin Fitzgerald, and Thomas Aarts "Siting Noxious Facilities: A Test of the Facility Siting Credo," *Risk Analysis* 13, no. 3 (1993): 301–318.

The way that "Guardians" look at risk is explained by Michael Elliott in Roy Lewicki, *Making Sense of Intractable Environmental Conflicts: Concepts and Cases* (Island Press, 2002), 295.

The Cape Wind story is described in Robert Whitcomb and Wendy Williams, *Cape Wind: Money, Celebrity, Class, Politics and the Battle for Our Energy Future on Nantucket Sound* (PublicAffairs, 2007).

The way mediation can be used to resolve facility siting disputes is described in Lawrence Susskind and Jeffrey Cruikshank, *Breaking the Impasse: Consensual Approaches to Resolving Public Disputes* (Basic Books, 1987).

The relationship between risk and justice is explained, along with when and how to use compensation, in Patrick Field, Howard Raiffa, and Lawrence Susskind, "Risk and Justice: Rethinking the Concept of Compensation," in *Annals of the American Academic of Political and Social Science* 545 (Sage Publications, 1996), 156–164.

Community benefits agreements (CBAs) are explained in "Empowering Communities Through Deliberation: The Model of Community Benefits Agreements," *Journal of Planning Education and Research* 27, no. 3 (2008): 261–276

CHAPTER 2. CREATE MORE VALUE: PROPOSE PACKAGES THAT ARE GOOD FOR THEM AND GREAT FOR YOU
Creating More Value through Trades
Value creation can be helped along in numerous ways by professional neutrals—facilitators or mediators. Examples of how this works are presented

in Lawrence Susskind and Jeffrey Cruikshank, *Breaking the Impasse: Consensual Approaches to Resolving Public Disputes* (Basic Books, 1987).

Negotiating Strategic Alliances
The Viatex Simulation is presented in detail in Hallam Movius and Lawrence Susskind, *Built to Win: Creating a World-Class Negotiating Organization* (Harvard Business Press, 2009), Appendix D, 185–189.

Managing Conflict within the Ranks
The various moves that managers can make to win support for their ideas internally are presented in Deborah Kolb and Judith Williams, *The Shadow Negotiation: How Women Can Master the Hidden Agendas That Determine Bargaining Success* (Simon and Schuster, 2000).

The differences between internal and external conflict are described in Hallam Movius and Lawrence Susskind, *Built to Win: Creating a World-Class Negotiating Organization* (Harvard Business Press, 2009).

When You Shouldn't Go It Alone
For a complete review of what we know about negotiating with agents and negotiating on behalf of someone else, see Robert Mnookin and Lawrence Susskind, eds., *Negotiating on Behalf of Others: Advice to Lawyers, Business Executives, Sports Agents, Diplomats, Politicians and Everybody Else* (Sage, 1999).

When a Majority Isn't Enough
My analysis of the shortcomings of majoritarian decision making is contained in Lawrence Susskind and Jeffrey Cruikshank, *Breaking Robert's Rules of Order: The New Way to Run Your Meeting, Build Consensus and Get Results* (Oxford University Press, 2006). The Spanish version of the book, written with Francisco Ingouville and published in 2011 in Buenos Aires by Granica, was titled *When a Majority Isn't Enough*.

CHAPTER 3. EXPECT THE UNEXPECTED: USE CONTINGENT OFFERS TO CLAIM MORE THAN THE OTHER SIDE
The Art of the Improviser
My discussion of the importance of improvisation in negotiation is based on Michael Wheeler and Lakshmi Balachandra, "What Negotiators Can

Learn from Improv Comedy," *Negotiation* 9, no. 8 (August 2006): 1–3. Subsequently, Michael Wheeler published *The Art of Negotiation: How to Improvise Agreements in a Chaotic World* (Simon and Schuster, 2013).

Talking to Climate Change Skeptics
The scientific debate about the sources and scope of climate change is ongoing. The short status report on where things stand at present that I like the best is Naomi Oreskes, "The Scientific Consensus on Climate Change," *Science* 3 306, no. 5702 (2004): 1,686. If you really want to dig into the myths and rebuttals about global warming, see Skeptical Science, "Global Warming & Climate Change Myths" (2013), www.skeptical science.com/argument.php.

My own take on the importance of taking climate change risk into account in all current decisions is presented in Lawrence Susskind, "Responding to the Risks Posed by Climate Change: Cities Have No Choice But to Adapt," *Town Planning Review* 81, no. 3 (2010): 217–235.

There are successful ways of engaging the public at large in decisions about how best to manage the risks associated with climate change. These are described in Lawrence Susskind and Evan Paul, "Winning Public Support for Addressing Climate Change," *The Solutions Journal* 1, no. 2 (2010): 44–48.

Don't Like Surprises? Use Contingent Agreements
Contingent agreements are described in more detail in Lawrence Susskind and Jeffrey Cruikshank, *Breaking Robert's Rules of Order: The New Way to Run Your Meeting, Build Consensus and Get Results* (Oxford University Press, 2006).

Self-enforcing agreements are explained in Lawrence S. Bacow and Michael Wheeler, *Environmental Dispute Resolution* (Springer, 1984).

What's Special about Technology-Related and Other Kinds of Complex Negotiations?
The Hexiglass case was created by my colleagues Beth Doherty and Hallam Movius for the Technology Negotiation Executive Training Program offered by the Public Disputes Program at the Program on Negotiation (PON) at Harvard Law School. The simulation can be downloaded from the PON Clearinghouse at www.pon.org.

The idea of strategic realignment was introduced by Joel Cutcher-Gershenfeld in his book with Robert McKersie and Richard Walton, *Pathways to Change: Case Studies in Strategic Labor Negotiations* (W. E. Upjohn Press, 1995).

CHAPTER 4. WRITE THEIR VICTORY SPEECH: HELP THE OTHER SIDE SELL YOUR BEST DEAL TO THEIR BACK TABLE
Build Both Offensive and Defensive Coalitions
The literature on coalitions and coalitional behavior is reviewed in great detail in Lawrence Susskind and Larry Crump, *Multiparty Negotiations*, 4 volumes (Sage, 2010).

James Sebenius explains the importance of sequencing in his article "Sequencing to Build Coalitions: With Whom Should I Talk First?" in *Wise Choices: Decisions, Games and Negotiations*, ed. Richard Zekhauser, Ralph Keeney, and James Sebenius (Harvard Business Press, 1996), 324–348.

For a summary of the WTO meeting in Cancún, see Anup Shah, "WTO Meeting in Cancún, Mexico, 2003, Global Issues, September 18, 2003, http://www.globalissues.org/article/438/wto-meeting-in-cancun-mexico-2003.]

Irwin Janis, *Groupthink: Psychological Studies of Policy Decisions and Fiascos* (Houghton-Mifflin, 1982).

The impact of groupthink on groups engaged in collaborative problem solving is nicely described in Deborah Ancona, Ray Friedman, and Deborah Kolb, "The Group and What Happens on the Way to 'Yes,'" *Negotiation Journal* 7, no. 1 (1991): 155–173.

Negotiating with Regulators
My ideas on this subject, with quite a few examples, are summarized in Lawrence Susskind, Paul Levy, and Jennifer Thomas-Larmer, *Negotiating Environmental Agreements: How to Avoid Escalation, Confrontation, Needless Cost and Expensive Litigation* (Island Press, 1999).

For more on how regulators think about and use discretion, see Lawrence Susskind and Joshua Secunda, "The Risks and Advantages of Agency Discretion: Evidence from EPA's Project XL," *UCLA Journal of Environmental Law and Policy* 17, no. 1: (1999): 67–116.

Mediation as Problem Solving

For more on mediation as problem solving, see Chester Crocker, Fen Osler Hampson, and Pamela Aall, *Taming Intractable Conflicts: Mediation in the Hardest Cases* (United States Institute of Peace Press, 2004).

For a complete description and discussion of how the Organization for Economic Cooperation and Development (OECD) has incorporated problem-solving mediation into its operations see *NCP Mediation Manual* (including the relevant texts from the OECD Guidelines as of February 12, 2012), Consensus Building Institute, http://www.cbuilding.org/publication/case/helping-oecd-ncps-use-mediation-implement-guidelines-multinational-enterprises.

One of the best books on mediation is Christopher Moore, *The Mediation Process: Practical Strategies for Resolving Conflicts* (Jossey-Bass, 2003).

CHAPTER 5. PROTECT YOURSELF: INSULATE AGREEMENTS AGAINST PREDICTABLE SURPRISES
Bringing Talks Back on Track with Facilitation
Sandy Shuman, *Creating a Culture of Collaboration: The International Association of Facilitators Handbook* (John Wiley, 2006).

Roger Schwarz, *The Skilled Facilitator: A Comprehensive Resource for Consultants, Facilitators, Managers, Trainers and Coaches* (John Wiley, 2002).

Michael Doyle and David Straus, *How to Make Meetings Work* (Berkeley Books, 1976).

Dispute Prevention: It's a Good Idea, Right?
The International Institute for Conflict Prevention and Resolution in New York City has published a series of dispute prevention reports. See "Reducing Disputes Through Wise Prevention Processes in Business Agreements" (undated).

Max Bazerman and Michael Watkins, *Predictable Surprises: The Disasters You Should Have Seen Coming, and How to Prevent Them* (Harvard Business Press, 2008).

For more on the design of dispute handling systems, see Nancy Rogers, Robert Bordone, Frank Sander, and Craig McEwen. *Designing Systems and Processes for Managing Disputes* (Aspen, 2013).

What to Do When the Other Person Is Lying
Howard Raiffa explains the difference between negotiating in a context in which full, open truthful exchange is occurring versus situations in which only partially open and truthful exchange is occurring in his *Three Lectures on Negotiation Analysis* (Program on Negotiation at Harvard Law School, 1996).

The ethics of negotiation are presented in detail in Carrie Menkel-Meadow and Michael Wheeler, eds., *What's Fair: Ethics for Negotiators* (Jossey-Bass, 2010).

Mediation ethics are discussed in Ellen Waldman, *Mediation Ethics: Cases and Commentaries* (Jossey-Bass, 2011).

CHAPTER 6. PROVIDE LEADERSHIP: BUILD YOUR ORGANIZATION'S NEGOTIATING CAPABILITIES

The Responsibilities of Leadership
Some of the most insightful ideas about leadership are in Ronald Heifitz, *Leadership without Easy Answers* (Harvard University Press, 1998).

Lawrence Susskind, "Build Expert Negotiators: What Do We Know about Training World-Class Negotiators," in *The Change Champion's Field Guide: Strategies and Tools for Leading Change in Your Organization*, ed. Louis Carter et al. (John Wiley, 2013).

When an Angry Public Wants to Be Heard
The strategies discussed in this section first appeared in Lawrence Susskind and Patrick Field, *Dealing with an Angry Public: The Mutual Gains Approach to Resolving Public Disputes* (Free Press, 1996).

For the best instruction regarding handling media pressure, see Jeffrey Ansell, *When the Headline Is YOU: An Insider's Guide to Handling the Media* (Jossey-Bass, 2010).

Helping Decentralized Organizations Negotiate More Effectively
Flatter, or decentralized, organizations strive to eliminate as many layers of middle management as they can. They rely on self-organizing teams and substantial employee involvement. They also give more responsibility to junior or entry-level employees and rely on rapid feedback to make continuous corrections and improvements.

Don't Get Lost in Translation
Kevin Avruch, an anthropologist at George Mason University has been writing about cross-cultural negotiation for quite some time. See, for example, his book *Culture and Conflict Resolution* (United States Institute for Peace, 1998).

In 1997 Raymond Cohen substantially revised his 1991 book, *Negotiating Across Cultures: International Communication in an Interdependent World* (U.S. Institute for Peace, 1997).

Edward and Mildred Hall, cultural anthropologists, were among the first to write about cultural differences in negotiating style. Their books *Hidden Differences: Doing Business with the Japanese, The Hidden Dimension*, and *Understanding Cultural Differences: Germans, French and Americans*, were all published in 1990 by Anchor Publishing. While they contain some ideas that no longer make sense in today's interdependent world, they were among the first to spell out the need to be sensitive to cultural differences when we negotiate.

Linguistic relatively, or the Sapir-Whorf hypothesis, has been written about by many people, especially June H. Hill and Bruce Mannheim in "Language and World View," which appeared in the *Annual Review of Anthropology* 21 (1992): 381–406. Although there is much debate about it, the hypothesis presumes that differences in the way languages encode cultural and cognitive categories affect the way people think. This means that people who speak different languages will probably think and behave differently, depending on the languages they use.

Negotiating for Continuous Improvement
For more on this subject, see Hallam Movius and Lawrence Susskind, *Built to Win: Creating a World-Class Negotiating Organization* (Harvard Business Press, 2009).

For a more complete discussion of the pros and cons of investing in negotiation training, see Hallam Movius and Lawrence Susskind, *Built to Win: Creating a World-Class Negotiating Organization* (Harvard Business Press, 2009).

Kurt Lewin, "Frontiers in Group Dynamics: II. Channels of Group Life; Social Planning and Action Research," *Human Relations* 1, no. 2 (1947): 143–153.

Patricia Phillips and John Phillips, "11 Reasons Why Training and Development Fails . . . and What You Can Do About It," *Training* 39 (2002): 78–85.

D. L. Kirkpatrick, "Techniques for Evaluating Training Programs," *Journal of the ASTD* 13 (1959: 3–9).

The Importance of Good Negotiation Coaching
The dynamics of negotiation coaching are described further in Hallam Movius and Lawrence Susskind, *Built to Win: Creating a World-Class Negotiating Organization* (Harvard Business Press, 2009).

CODA: FINDING THE SWEET SPOT IN YOUR NEXT NEGOTIATION

Roger Fisher, William Ury, and Bruce Patton, *Getting to Yes: Negotiating Agreement Without Giving In* (Penguin, 1991).

Howard Raiffa, *The Art and Science of Negotiation* (Belknap, 1985).

Howard Raiffa, John Richardson, and David Metcalfe, *Negotiation Analysis: The Science and Art of Collaborative Decision Making* (Belknap, 2003).

In thinking about the location of the sweet spot in any negotiation, I drew on Noah G. Susskind, "Wiggle Room: Rethinking Reservation Values in Negotiation," *Ohio State Journal on Dispute Resolution* Volume 26, No 1 (2011): 79–117.

Global environmental treaty making dynamics are described in more detail in my book Lawrence Susskind, *Environmental Diplomacy: Negotiating More Effective Global Agreements* (Oxford University Press, 1996).

The distinction between empathy and assertiveness in negotiation is developed in Robert H. Mnookin, Scott R. Peppet, and Andrew S. Tulumello, "The Tension Between Empathy and Assertiveness," *Negotiation Journal* 12, no. 3 (July 1996): 217–230.

INDEX

Lawrence Susskind is Ford Foundation Professor of Urban and Environmental Planning at the Massachusetts Institute of Technology, where he has been a member of the faculty for more than forty years. He is also founder and Chief Knowledge Officer of the Consensus Building Institute, a not-for-profit mediation firm that provides consensus-building assistance in some of the most complicated disputes around the world. He helped to create the inter-university Program on Negotiation at Harvard Law School, where he is currently vice-chair and provides advanced executive training.

Professor Susskind has mediated numerous disputes, including regulatory conflicts, facility siting controversies, public policy disagreements, and confrontations between corporations. He has served as a court-appointed special master and helped facilitate multilateral global environmental treaty negotiations. He has served as a guest lecturer at more than two-dozen universities around the world, and he is the author or co-author of sixteen books, many of which have been published in multiple languages.